the **Reputation** *game*

the **Reputation** *game*

PETER ROPER

LESLEY MORRISSEY

bookshaker

First Published in Great Britain
2013 by www.BookShaker.com

Contents

Introduction

You never get a second chance to make a first impression

We all talk of a 'good game'; we all mean well, but how good are we really and how much attention do we pay to our reputations on a daily or even hourly basis? Do we walk the talk?

We have to put our hands up – even we don't do everything right. However, there's a big case for awareness. If you don't know what you're doing – right or wrong – you can't improve things.

A century ago information travelled slowly – and a century before that even slower. The time it took for a message to get from A to B could be days, or even weeks and months. Since Tim Berners Lee invented the internet in the 1980s, information goes round the world in seconds.

In today's world we take it for granted that we can talk to virtually anyone in any country, not just from our offices, but from our homes and from our pockets with phones that have more computing power than the entire NASA space programme did in the 1960s.

In a generation life has shifted dramatically. Our access to each other is just one aspect of the internet's impact. It also gives us access to information, not all of it accurate – but mostly, easy to check out. These two together mean that, in a heartbeat, you can go from hero to zero if you're not paying attention.

Old thinking doesn't do it anymore; you have to play the reputation game, whether you like it or not.

As we wrote this book the 2012 Olympics were in full flow and the Olympic ideal – the spirit of sportsmanship – is a great example of what happens when people get it right. It changed the way a whole nation was perceived, not least by their own nationals!

However, some things did go wrong: a journalist criticising an athlete who didn't sing the national anthem; negative messages about athletes being broadcast on Twitter; demands for a drugs test when a young girl swam faster than anyone expected. It always leaves a bad taste in everyone's mouth when high ideals are brought crashing down and, as a result, some*one*'s – or some country's – reputation can be permanently damaged by something as careless as a mis-posted tweet.

Why did we write this book?

Quite simply, because it's a subject we are both passionate about. We've seen people get it right and do really well; we've seen people get it spectacularly wrong and been wiped out, or had to struggle for a long time to be taken seriously.again in their industry.

We have a question for you first:

How serious are you – REALLY?

If you are just dabbling, then this book is probably not for you. If you don't want to play, don't read any further. If you go to a seminar and then don't take action on what you've learned, we're probably not your kind of people!

However, if you want to really get it right, you must be prepared to take it seriously. If you think it's important to manage your reputation, then we hope you'll find plenty of useful ammunition in the pages that follow.

Where are you at in creating and managing your reputation? Are you just thinking about it, or have you arrived at the planning or taking action stage?

What this book IS

This book will give you plenty to get your teeth into – and a few things to think about. By the time you've got to the end you will have everything you need to develop and create a first class reputation (and, perhaps, plug the odd gap).

If you are one of those people who want to get down to it super-fast, there is a plan in Chapter 13. However, we recommend that you do the job properly and start with Section One, which gives you an overview and a host of tools and techniques you can apply to yourself and your organisation.

Section Two provides you with a guide on how to start managing your reputation. We have advice for sole traders, independent consultants, small businesses, corporate organisations and social enterprises. You'll pick up some useful tips if you read all the chapters – but our intention is that you read the one that is most appropriate to your business.

We've written the book in a conversational style. It can be picked up and put down, referred to when necessary and, if you like, scribbled in, highlighted and underlined. If you're reading on an electronic device of some kind, make sure you have a notepad handy to jot down your thoughts as you go.

What this book ISN'T

It's *not* a guide to deal with the media[1]. Most people don't have to think about being interviewed on TV, radio or for the press, although in today's world you are making your own news, so a knowledge of how the media works isn't a bad thing to have.

It isn't technical – it's straightforward and all advice that anyone can follow – if they choose to.

It's not going to tell you what your reputation should be. There are different perceptions of each of us; some people are great in some people's eyes, but not so great in the opinions of others (consider any politician). The aim is that you should aim to be consistently the best you can be.

In the end, nobody can do this for you – it's down to you. How important is your reputation to you? That's the million-dollar question.

---

[1] If you need advice on that we couldn't do better than recommend our good friend Alan Stevens, The Media Coach.

Section 1

HOW REPUTATION MANAGEMENT WORKS

CHAPTER 1

What is reputation?

Almost everybody is concerned about their reputation.

Most of us are keen to have a good one for a wide variety of reasons – from wanting to impress our peers to influencing potential employers or clients.

Some people cultivate a bad reputation to intimidate the people they want to control.

Everyone is anxious to ensure their reputation is maintained and remains undamaged as far as possible – although they may not admit it. How many times have you heard someone say 'I don't care what people say about me'? You may have said it yourself – but most of us do care, especially about how those people see us who we are close to or want on our side.

So, what is reputation? Is it what we do? What we say? How we behave? *The Oxford English Dictionary* defines 'reputation' as *the beliefs or opinions that are generally held about someone or something. Also as a widespread belief that someone or something has a particular characteristic.*

Wikipedia says: **Reputation** *of a social entity (a person, a group of people or an organisation) is an opinion about that entity, typically a result of social evaluation on a set of criteria. It is important in education, business, and online communities.*

Reputation may be considered as a component of the identity as defined by others.

Quite simply, reputation is really **what people say about us.**

What have you heard?

You already have impressions of organisations and individuals that are famous or you know.

Let's play a game.

Think of 10 world-famous organisations – and then give each one a score out of 10 – one being poor reputation and 10 being universally top notch.

1.

2.

3.

4.

5.

6.

7.

8.

9.

10.

TIP: It's best to play this game on paper – we'll be asking you to think further about your answers. Plenty of paper to scribble on and a pen or pencil is definitely going to be useful as you read this book.

Now do the same for famous people. Famous business people, film stars, pop personalities, TV presenters or actors – anyone you like. Mark them out of 10 for their reputation, too.

1.

2.

3.

4.

5.

6.

7.

8.

9.

10.

Bring this closer to home with companies that you know – ones that you have heard about locally or with whom you have done business. Do the same exercise: list 10 and rate their reputations based on what you have heard or know.

1.

2.

3.

4.

5.

6.

7.

8.

9.

10.

Did you struggle to think of 10 companies? Did you find companies with good or bad reputations were easier to think of? Hold that thought!

The last group to list are people you know. Think about individuals that you actually know, whether they are business owners, people you have seen presenting training or seminars, people you know through networking, friends and family.

1.

2.

3.

4.

5.

6.

7.

8.

9.

10.

We all know lots of people; they're around us every day, at home, at work, where we socialise, at meetings, training sessions, in shops and offices. In fact, you probably found it hard to know who to put on your list and who to leave out. You may even have found your list has sneaked past that number 10 we mentioned earlier! Don't worry. If it has, nobody's checking.

Now you should have four lists, with a rating next to every entry. The next bit in the game is harder, but give it some thought. Let's make it a bit easier – take the organisations or individuals with the highest and lowest rating on each list and jot down what made you rate them high or low.

- What have you heard about them?
- What have they done that makes you feel they deserve the rating you've given them?
- Is this a personal view or is it fairly universal – as in, do you think most people would agree with your opinion?

This is probably going to take you some time – and some of your answers will be harder to pin down than others. Well-known organisations and celebrities are probably easier as there is plenty of press coverage and factual data to support your choices. The people and companies around you are usually harder to describe as your opinion will be much more subjective.

How are you doing?

Let's look at our own lists:

Worldwide organisations	Rating	Reason for rating
1. Virgin	9	Inspirational, modern, exciting
2. Apple	9	Leading edge, state-of-the-art, new, funky
3. BBC	7	Respectable, reliable, good quality
4. Mars	8	Great employer, cares about staff, change leader
5. Cadburys	7	Family oriented, community based (would have been higher before they 'sold out' to Kraft)
6. Tiffanys	8	High quality, fabulous jewellery, premium, luxury items
7. Microsoft	5	Good products, but known for glitches and using the public to iron them out, feeling that they're taking over
8. Comic Relief	9	Involvement, good cause, enthusiasm, fun, can see the difference made with donations
9. Facebook	8	Fun, friendly, maintaining connections, making friends, lots to do, easy to use, the challenges that they experienced when they put Facebook on the stockmarket, haven't changed the platform itself – it's still enormously popular for keeping up with friends and family as well as a great place for companies to stay in touch with their customers.
10. Go Compare	4/7	We couldn't agree on this, Lesley thinks it's an irritating advert that creates a negative influence for a useful service. Peter thinks it's fun and amusing. Now the advertising agency have taken it a step further where they blow up the irritating opera singer – obviously responding to the irritated masses. However, great adverts don't make a reputation alone (except, perhaps for the agency).

Remember that this was our list and there's no right or wrong – the lists are very subjective, as our response to number 10 demonstrates. These numbers change depending on circumstances, incoming information and even what's happened to you on any particular day; for instance, whilst you may love Cadbury's chocolate, if you're embarking on a diet, your view of it is likely to be less rosy!

We noticed that our list was predominantly positive; organisations we felt good about. What about yours? Were there common themes that emerged?

Our next list for high profile people:

Worldwide organisations	Rating	Reason for rating
1. Richard Branson	9	He is everything Virgin stands for – an adventurer, someone who bucks the establishment and succeeds
2. Steve Jobs	6	From a business point of view – brilliant; should be a 10, but his personal reputation is perceived by many as not so great[2].
3. Bill Gates	8	Whilst Microsoft is taking over the world, Bill Gates has invested a huge amount of his fortune in a charitable trust and is trying to do his bit to help the disadvantaged. His personal reputation has improved as a result.
4. Barack Obama	7	Seems to be pragmatic, demonstrates he has a sense of humour, appears to be dedicated to a difficult job. Having a wife that the media loves and who knows exactly how to please them, contributes to his reputation too; perhaps we are a sum of our parts!
5. Amy Winehouse	6	Amazing artist, but her addictions flawed her image.
6. Simon Cowell	7	Whether you love or hate him, he is undeniably successful and has charisma.
7. Terry Wogan	9	Warm and 'cuddly' image, doesn't take himself too seriously and leads the Children in Need annual charity drive. Despite a setback when it was revealed he was paid a substantial sum for his work with Children in Need, he has recovered ground and continues to support the charity without receiving large fees.
8. Anthony Robbins	6	Very subjective – some people would make this a 10. His message is powerful and positive, his delivery isn't our style.
9. Rupert Murdoch	4	Whilst enormously successful, the media has ensured his image is now tarnished forever.
10. David Beckham	9	Football fans love him for his undeniable sports skill, others like his self-effacing personality and dedication to doing things that are good for the community. Even though he lives in the USA he still makes an effort to 'be there' for the British public – his football academy and his very active support of the London 2012 Olympics.

People are often harder to rate – there's more emotion invested in a person than an organisation. This makes the opinions far more

---

[2] If you want to know more read Walter Isaacson's book *Steve Jobs: The Exclusive Biography*

subjective. We know several people who have avid fans and equally strong adversaries: the Marmite factor!

What makes you an avid fan?

On your lists of companies and people you know there will almost certainly be those of whom you are an avid fan. The reasons for them being there are usually more to do with their attitude than their competence.

PETER'S STORY

Why did I drive 35 miles out of my way a few weeks ago to go to a tyre bay when these services were available much nearer to home?

I've been going to A44 Tyres[3] for 15 years, originally recommended by someone else and they were closer to where I used to live. The first time I took the car in I said 'I think it probably needs four new tyres'.

'No,' they said. 'You only need two.'

I was staggered because I had worked with the motor industry for many years and I know that lots of stories are true – but there are some very good companies.

A44 Tyres in Worcester have never let me down – and they've been exactly the same with umpteen people that I've sent to them over the years. They never rip you off; they just do the job right.

Their reputation is renowned throughout Worcestershire.

What about you?

Let's turn this around and look at you and your business.

Now we're getting to the point where it's really difficult for you to be objective. Most of us only know what people tell us and it can be hard to differentiate between flattery and objective feedback!

It's time for some tough questions! Get the paper and pen out and jot down your answers.

---

[3] If you'd like to find out how good their service is you'll find them at www.a44tyreshop.co.uk

Tough question one – what about your business?

You've worked hard to establish a business and most of us want it to be a respected company that people are happy to recommend. How do you currently rate your business? This is your personal opinion.

1	2	3	4	5	6	7	8	9	10

You'll have had some feedback if you've been in business for a year or two so:

How do you think others rate your business?

What do your clients, competitors, business associates and suppliers think about your business?

1	2	3	4	5	6	7	8	9	10

If you've got lots of testimonials from your clients about how great they think you are that's a good start, but if all your clients were asked to carry out the rating exercise you've just done do you think that:

- You'd be on their list as one of the first companies/people they thought of?
- Your rating would be 8 or above?

Assuming you're on their list what would their comments be about you and your company? Do you think that their comments and ratings would be what you'd like them to be?

Tough question two – do you get a good personal rating?

As a small business you may be in the situation where you *are* the business. As the business grows, people may know the business, but not necessarily all the people within it. If you lead or work for a large organisation your personal reputation will have an impact on your employer and influence the people who work for you, if you are a manager. If you had to assess your personal reputation how would you rate yourself?

1	2	3	4	5	6	7	8	9	10

Let's go back to all those people who know you personally – how would they rate you?

These are the people you do business with – suppliers, clients, staff, competitors and people you've met on the business networking circuit.

1	2	3	4	5	6	7	8	9	10

This is a good point to reflect on the answers to those two questions. If there's a gap between what people think and say and what you'd like them to think and say, it's time to start putting together a plan to build your reputation further.

Tough question three – what creates reputation?

If you're just starting a business then your reputation is likely to be almost non-existent – there needs to be something to base it on, a track record, some kind of information or evidence, either factual or anecdotal.

For most new businesses a third-party association is the best way to start until your own business's reputation is established. This is known as *social proof*, e.g. if you're selling electronics, using Bose speakers will immediately mark you out as good quality. If you've been around a few years then your reputation should be reasonably well-developed.

Unsolicited testimonials are evidence that your clients are happy with the work or products you've provided, but reputation is built on what people say in conversation, whether face-to-face, on the phone or in e-mails and other communications. **It's what people are saying when you're not there.**

Testimonials play their part – and are really valuable; they can be the catalyst for a conversation about you and your business, but they won't create a good reputation on their own.

When you were working on the lists of companies and people you know, how many of the reasons for your rating were based on personal knowledge and how much on what people had said to you?

If you've ever attended networking meetings you will have met more than one accountant, for instance. You've heard what they have to say about their business approach, but how likely are they to appear on your list of 10 companies unless:

- They're your accountant and they're doing a great job?
- You've heard from someone else who is one of their clients and raves about how good they are?
- You've heard several people saying how good they are and what makes them better than the average accountant?

There are dozens of accountants, big and small, in your area. Most of them are competent or they wouldn't be in business, but what makes one stand out above the rest?

First-hand knowledge is invaluable, but it's not enough to build a reputation. Everyone should think their accountant is doing a great job (or they need to change accountants).

Hearing someone rave about how good their accountant is usually indicates there is something special about them as most of us don't get very excited about our accountants as long as they're doing the job they're supposed to. (Of course, we both have accountants we're happy to rave about!)

Hearing lots of people talk about the same accountant – especially when some of them are not (yet) their clients – indicates that there is something more than simply being good at what they do. They have a really good reputation.

So what creates reputation is, effectively, gossip!

Worldwide organisations

Every company has a culture – it's all about the way in which they approach their business and encompasses their attitude to:

- The quality of their product or services.

- Their customers.
- Their marketplace and competitors.
- Their staff.

Every big organisation started out as a small one and the way the company develops is usually down to the founder or partners. Their vision of how they want the company to operate will influence their policies and how they develop, create and deliver their products or services to the customer.

That's the foundation for their reputation – but that doesn't create a reputation.

Part of reputation building is marketing. If you're not making a noise nobody knows you're there!

Companies like Apple built their reputation on creating products that were dramatically different from anything their competitors produced. A lot of people loved their products, liked their approach and raved about them. Apple continued to deliver leading-edge innovative products and the news spread until the whole world had heard of them.

Marketing isn't just about having innovative products – it can also be about innovative advertising. When we see an advert we really like, we attach that liking to the brand. Over the years there are ads that create warm feelings about the product. Older readers will remember:

- Beanz meanz Heinz.
- The aliens who found instant mashed potato hysterically funny (Smash).
- The bubbles that had passed the Corona Fizzical.
- The Milk Tray man.
- The Big Green Giant.
- The Cadbury's Flake girls

Today's ads also create connections:

- Frustrated meerkats that have turned into more than just an advertising gimmick (CompareTheMarket.com).
- Gorgeous girls who admit to all kinds of flaws, but use a

product because 'we're worth it', encouraging us all to try to emulate their flowing tresses or flawless skin (L'Oreal).

- Werther's Originals with their cosy 'Grandfather's favourites' image (August Storck KG).

Clever advertising can turn an image around as people talk about the ad positively and start people viewing their image differently. Sometimes this works and sometimes it doesn't. For instance, BT have invested millions in an advertising campaign that is very human, personal and features a family from the time the couple got together as they grow, start a family and deal with their growing children. The Bisto family ran an ad series for years that was almost like a soap and very successful, as did Gold Blend coffee, but BT haven't managed to create the same loyalty.

Does it give BT a better reputation? Maybe for some people, but one bad experience at the hands of any of their staff will wipe all those good feelings away. Those people who have consistently poor experiences will have a completely different view.

Every ad creates an image of the product and the company behind it. We gossip about the big organisations through their advertising campaigns. However, today it's not just the TV and print media – social media has become an incredibly powerful reputation tool. It can enhance a company's reputation – or destroy it in just 140 characters.

Celebrities

Most high profile individuals understand the power of social media. Performers can engage with their fans quickly, easily and en-masse. Those who have 'got' Twitter have an edge as they can share their personal lives with a huge fan-base, creating that feeling of being close without actually meeting thousands of people.

However, the media can still make or break reputations – even their own, as Mr Murdoch (owner of News Corp International) is only too well aware after the phone hacking scandal that has gone on and on.

Celebrities who shun the media, or who are rude or aggressive, quickly gain a reputation for being difficult, no matter how talented they might be. Those who work with the media are much more likely to have a positive image. Even people who are not avid fans of a particular individual will form an opinion based on what they see on TV and in the press – or, these days, on YouTube.

Of course, people don't expect rock stars to behave like saints; they can get away with the occasional lapse: having too much to drink, or being seen snuggling up to someone they shouldn't. However, if you're a public figure you have to live up to expectations. There are always exceptions, but bucking the rules can backfire badly.

Politicians build their reputation on being highly visible and delivering strong messages. Of course, there are people who support their views and people who oppose them, but their reputations are built on how well they deliver both their message and their promises. However, if they fail to conduct themselves in the way we expect, their reputation tumbles.

A number of politicians have resigned because:

- They've had a relationship outside their marriage.
- They've been in a business relations.hip with someone inappropriate
- They've made comments that indicate they don't live up to the image they are presenting.
- They've cheated or appeared to cheat in some way (the expenses scandal that rocked British politics in 2011 affected all the parties).

It's often not so much about what they have said or done, but more about the fact that their judgment has been found wanting. If a politician is representing me I don't want them to have poor judgment – I won't trust them any longer.

Business people have the same issues to deal with.

Remember how badly the reputation of the banks was damaged by the activities of Fred Goodwin, former boss of the Royal Bank of Scotland – otherwise known as Fred the Shred (a nickname related to his ability to pare costs down).

His takeover of many other financial organisations turned RBS into a powerful bank (and won Fred a knighthood), but his judgment of when to stop was flawed, putting RBS into a situation where the UK government had to bail them out. The result was that his reputation was shredded.

He had to step down and the media couldn't get enough of his redundancy millions to the point where he was stripped of his knighthood.

In today's world, our opinions of celebrities are based on a combination of the talent they display – in whatever field they're in, the reports of their behaviour in the media along with what they say and what's said about them on social media.

No matter what you think, we all love the gossip!

Magazines like *OK* and *Hello* wouldn't survive otherwise and most of the glossies have celebrity 'interviews' that are featured on the cover to attract more readers. The celebs know that it's good for their reputations to be in these prime publications and sell the rights to their weddings, christenings and divorces to stay centre front in the public's vision.

Local organisations

These are not companies likely to be found in the international business news (although there may be one or two future world brands), but they are carving out a business in the local community.

Of course, they want a good reputation, or they won't survive. The question is who they want to know about them. For a local printer they need to be visible to all the local businesses. For manufacturers of a specialist piece of technology that is only useful to a very niche industry, evidence of their reputation needs to be in the place those potential clients are looking.

How do you get people talking about you – without them necessarily having to be your clients?

Small companies, like big ones, need to have a strong ethos and understand what their customers want. Then, they not only need to deliver what is wanted in the way it's wanted, but to find a way to stand out from their competitors. That's just **step one.**

Step two is to make sure as many people in the potential marketplace know about you – in other words, your marketing campaign.

Step three is to ensure that as much as possible about your company is positive. Even if someone has a complaint, the way in which you deal with it can result by affecting your reputation positively.

PETER'S STORY

The Professional Speaking Association Conference took place at one of Hilton's hotels last year. When we arrived on the Friday morning, we realised that many of our overseas visitors were unhappy to discover they had no soap in their room.

Former PSA President, Alan Stevens, stepped in and said: 'You go and have breakfast and I'll sort it out'.

He spoke to reception and they said: 'We've run out and won't get a delivery until Monday'. Alan made some suggestions (local supermarket), but couldn't get anywhere.

As a top media coach, Alan is no stranger to the power of the media and the internet; his Twitter following is huge. One tweet with the #Hilton hashtag soon put the world in the picture!

Before noon the General Manager of the hotel, who was on a day off, rang him to ask how she could help. Alan explained the situation and the manager promised to get it sorted out immediately (which she did).

She then asked what else she could do. Alan pointed out that it seemed unfair to penalise guests who were already paying for their room and food by charging them for the car park and also £15 per device, per day for internet access – one American couple were paying an additional £60 a day for two laptops and two smartphones.

The manager immediately agreed to waive all these charges for people attending the convention.

What did she want in return?

'If you could make a comment on Twitter that this has been resolved, that would be good.'

Individuals

When you're running a small business your personal reputation often is your business reputation. As small businesses grow, the hardest thing for some owners is to step back from doing everything themselves, simply because they feel that customers expect them to be hands on. That's how they've gained their reputation.

However, personal reputation can be separated from business reputation, as long as the business continues to deliver the same high quality products or services, in the same customer-focused way.

Gaining that personal reputation is a great start for a business and there are many things you can do to enhance your reputation.

Firstly, you need to be **visible**. If you look around your local area you'll see office buildings and commercial premises without any indication of the business that occupies them. **Get your brand up.**

Secondly, **get out and meet people**. Today there are a multitude of opportunities to network. If nobody has ever met you, it's unlikely that your reputation will grow much. Get out there and get to know people.

Thirdly, **help others**. Get a reputation as a connector. When your network grows, get into the habit of seeing possibilities for other people and make those connections. If someone needs help and you can give it, make the offer.

PETER'S STORY

Author of Recommended and my co-author of And Death Came Third, Andy Lopata and I met in Manchester and were in a hotel bar along with a group of people who had obviously been in there all day. Young couples moved away from the noisy crowd and came to sit next to us at the bar.

We got talking and Andy asked what they did. The young lady (who we discovered was called Natasha) confided that she was keen to find a job in advertising. Andy mentioned that his brother-in-law was a director of an advertising agency in London, the name of which caused Natasha some excitement.

'I can't just ask my brother-in-law if he will recruit you, but I am happy to ask him if he'll talk to you and give you some advice to help you find a position,' Andy volunteered.

He also offered to connect her with a well-known networker in the Manchester area to help her to make connections and made some other suggestions to help.

Natasha followed up with Andy by e-mail and he made the calls as promised.

Natasha attended a local networking breakfast as a result and made some really good contacts including someone who put her in touch with a company who were looking for a marketing person.

She met Andy's brother-in-law – and duly thanked him for his help. It didn't stop there. Andy called her a couple of weeks later to connect her to the friend of a friend who had just landed a new job in one of the biggest ad agencies in London, so she could find out how she did it!

Natasha was, as you can imagine, very grateful. You can be sure she will recommend Andy and his networking expertise every chance she gets.

THE POINT OF THIS CHAPTER
So what is reputation?

Everything you do contributes to your reputation – even the things you do that you don't think people notice. It's usually the things you think nobody is paying attention to that everyone ends up talking about. We all love a secret – and a scandal!

Networking involves plenty of gossip. Do small business owners gossip at their networking meetings? Of course they do!

Reputation is what people say about you – when you're not there. It's what's on the bush telegraph; it's gossip!

A good reputation is more valuable than money.

PUBLILIUS SYRUS

CHAPTER 2

Why is reputation important?

Even as a child you learned about reputation. Remember your parents told you – 'don't hang around with...'? And it was all because of that child's reputation – or maybe that of his or her parents.

Regardless of how much people may say, 'I don't care what people say about me,' most of us do care; especially if what is being said is having an effect on your lifestyle and image.

What people say can influence decision making at every level.

In your local community what would you think about:

- A neighbour who is frequently heard screaming at their children?
- An old person who complains all the time about people parking in 'their' space in a crowded street?
- A councillor who didn't take action to lobby against a telephone mast being erected right next to a group of houses?
- A neighbour who always says 'good morning' when they're out walking their dog?
- A shopkeeper who is friendly and helpful?

Your opinion about each of these people will shape their reputation, but only when you discuss it with others. We've both experienced all of these – and we definitely have opinions about the 'perpetrators'.

It might affect your willingness to take action when they need help too. If you've formed a negative opinion, either through first-hand experience, or as a result what you've heard from others in the community, your inclination to do something is likely to be far less. If you see them in a more positive light you'll be much more likely to want to help.

Business is business

It doesn't matter what type of business you are in – your reputation may be the first contact other people have with your business.

We've all had good and bad experiences that we've passed on to others. Peter's A44 Tyres is a good example of a positive experience. Here's a less positive example.

LESLEY'S STORY

I once visited a local café with a friend for lunch. We had made an impulsive decision and sat down at their tables in the courtyard and looked at the menu. Quite soon someone came to take our order.

'I'll have the sausage with onion gravy and mash,' I said.

'I'm sorry, but we don't have any sausages at present, so that's not available.'

I couldn't believe what I was hearing as we were in a little local shopping precinct with a butcher's shop about a dozen feet away from where we were sitting and a supermarket about 50 feet away.

I said I'd wait if they had to nip out and buy sausages, but the waitress said 'We can't do that'. No explanation – and I knew that this wasn't a franchise or chain with buying policies (not that this should have made a difference).

Reluctantly, I chose something else on the menu. It wasn't exceptional and my friend's meal wasn't what he expected. Ham, egg and chips turned out to be a slice of boiled ham – not the ham steak he had been looking forward to.

We tried to talk to the owner before we left, but she really didn't want to know and said – I don't lie – 'You can't please some people'.

Needless to say, we've both told a lot of people about our negative experience and, I have to admit, I experienced a little satisfaction when the business was sold to someone else a year or so later.

The sad thing is that we talk more about negative experiences than good ones.

Studies have shown consistently over several decades that most of us tell between eight and 25 people about a bad service experience. We only tell one or two people about a good experience.

This may seem unfair, but we expect to get reasonable service so when we do, we don't consider it exceptional – just what we were expecting. In order for service to stand out it has to be much better than we were expecting.

If your first connection with a potential customer is how someone else talks about you then you really want that to be a good experience for them.

Imagine people chatting at a networking meeting:

'I've just moved to this area and I'm looking for a decent printer, do you know anyone?'

'Yes, you should try Print Superbly; I've heard they're quite good.'

Not exactly a glowing recommendation – but not bad either. If the response had been:

'Oh yes, you couldn't do better than Print Superbly. They're really helpful – and very quick. You need to talk to Joe – let me dig his number out for you.'

Do you think that would be a better recommendation? How about if the response had been:

'I always use Print Superbly, they're not the cheapest, but their quality and service are amazing and they're worth every penny'?

You don't want people talking about you in a lukewarm way. You want people to be hearing enthusiastic responses and be eager to talk about you and your business in a very positive way.

It doesn't matter how good you are; if people don't know that, it won't build the reputation you need for your business to flourish.

There are many very competent people around – but they aren't necessarily at the top of their professions, simply because not enough people know about them and talk about them. In business 'quietly competent' is not necessarily a good thing! In other words, good gossip is worthwhile when others speak of you – and when you speak of others.

When reputation = profit

Take the average accounts department – their focus is on ensuring the numbers stack up. Suggest they give away something that is going to cost the company money in order to enhance the reputation and they'll argue that you can't measure the outcomes – and, therefore, it's not a good idea!

Bean counters are usually only interested in how many pounds will come in as a result of the pounds given out. They can't always see the importance of a good reputation – because they can't see how to measure it in pounds (or dollars or euros).

In order for them to be convinced you need to provide them with examples:

How much did Richard Branson's ballooning adventures cost Virgin?

How much did his image as an adventurer and inspiring leader add to Virgin's bottom line?

How much does a TV advertisement for a new product cost?

How many people buy that product in favour of a non-advertising competitor's product as a result of that ad?

How much does your attendance at a networking group cost your company?

How many people have become customers as a result of many people knowing you and recommending you to the people they know?

It's difficult to measure the results – but, you can be sure that there are positive ones.

We know of more than one person who has found networking really successful for them – to the point where they have got so busy they have no longer had time to attend networking events. After a few months their business starts to drop off – and they can't work out what the problem is.

Miraculously, if they start networking again, things turn around gradually.

So what has this got to do with reputation?

That's simple – if people don't see you, it's easy to forget about you, especially if they know other people who are in the same business. Call it being fickle if you like, but most of us don't run around with a directory of all the people we know and what they do in our heads. Yes, we may have a business card from a single meeting six months back, but that doesn't help when someone asks for a referral to a suitable company.

This is why networking groups where you meet the same people many times can work well – you get to know each other better and learn more about the products and services each business offers. Your ability to recommend a company increases with your knowledge of that person and their business.

Unfortunately, if they disappear off the scene, we soon forget.

What happens when you have a good reputation?

If you remember *The Man with the Golden Gun* and the famous quote: 'Your reputation precedes you, Mr Bond', you'll know what we're talking about.

When you meet someone for the first time and they say 'Oh yes, I've heard about you,' your knee-jerk reaction may be 'I hope it was good'. It usually is good news; as it means that people have been saying good things about you.

People want to deal with someone that they have heard good things about. It means they don't have to do lots of research into the company before embarking on a relationship.

Of course, if you're a big organisation and you're about to spend large sums of money with a new supplier, you must do due diligence – however, to even be in the running can rest on each company's reputation.

If there's a choice of half a dozen possible suppliers and three have excellent reputations, two don't seem to have anything positive or negative and you've heard rumours about the sixth, it makes good business sense to start with the first three. Why make the effort to find out if there's any truth in the rumour or have to dig to find out how good the other two are?

So a good reputation opens doors that would otherwise remain firmly closed (and sometimes locked).

What happens when your reputation is damaged?

A damaged reputation is a liability. Usually it's the result of something you've done or said; occasionally it's damaged by things beyond your control, such as a hate campaign by a disgruntled customer or ex-member of staff.

Let's look at something most of us can relate to – cars. Cars tend to generate emotion and reflect their owners and their aspirations. When a car manufacturer tries to change their image, they are at risk of alienating their existing customers, who have bought that make for a reason – the reputation they had in the first place.

A good example is Mercedes. They used to be known for being high quality, despite being solid and a bit boring. Then they decided to try to emulate the companies they saw as their competitors: BMW and Audi. They tried to create a more sexy and exciting image and, in the process, lost the plot on quality. Their reputation has slipped and Volvo has stepped up to take over their solid, reliable reputation.

One of the biggest setbacks they experienced was when they launched the A Class – and road tests rapidly proved the vehicle to be unstable when cornering. That made the world news and they had to go back to the drawing board before releasing the model again.

Mercedes used to be a no-brainer first choice for quality – they topped the JD power surveys – but now it's down the list somewhere with lots of question marks beside the brand. It remains to be seen whether their reputation for quality is recoverable and what they might do about it.

Most of us would never deliberately damage the reputation of our company (or ourselves), but sometimes it's easy to open our mouths without putting the brain in gear.

FOR EXAMPLE

High Street jeweller, H Samuel, was once owned by the family business, Ratners.

But, when its boss stood up at the Institute of Directors (IoD) in 1991 and declared a sherry decanter that was part of Samuel's gift line to be 'total crap', it was instantly seized upon by the media.

It was estimated that £500m was wiped from the value of the company, Gerald Ratner lost his job and is remembered mostly for his 'foot-in-mouth' skills.

His comments weren't confined to sherry decanters. He also said a pair of earrings, priced at 99p were 'cheaper than a prawn sandwich from Marks & Spencer, but probably wouldn't last as long'.

Gerald Ratner is still selling jewellery – although considerably more up-market items – on the internet, but he spent nearly 15 years trying to recover his reputation and the business never recovered.

Reputation is based on trust and, like trust, takes time to establish – and a moment to destroy.

Whether you claim to care what people say about you or not, if you have a damaged reputation it will affect your ability to earn money in your chosen business.

If it's your personal reputation, people will not want to deal with you. They won't trust you.

If it's your business's reputation, it will affect not only you personally, but all the people who work in the business. Who wants to work for an organisation with a bad reputation?

Problems can enhance your reputation

It's a well-known fact that customers who have a problem sorted out are likely to be much more loyal customers than those who have never had a problem.

So why would having a problem sorted out make that much difference? Simply because the company has demonstrated how much they care about the customer and their needs.

When a company has made a real effort the customer – and the people that the customer talks to – gets a picture of an organisation that is human (we all make mistakes), but is willing to make a big effort to make the customer happy. That's the kind of organisation we all want to be served by.

Recognising where there's a negative image is the first step – and being brave enough to be up front in admitting there is a problem goes a long way towards keeping the customer on board.

Let's be honest, when a service provider starts making excuse after excuse about a problem, we lose interest. *They* know it's an excuse and *we* know it's an excuse. All we want to do is disengage.

However, when a company is brave enough – and honest enough – to say 'Whoops, we've made a boo-boo, we're sorry. Now what can we do to put it right?' we're likely to respect them more and be willing to listen to what they're offering to do to sort things out (remember the Hilton experience in Chapter 1?)

When your reputation is in the cheap and cheerful (and not very reliable) category, changing that perception can seem impossible, but it's been done – and very successfully.

I have a Skoda. I bought it second-hand from my brother earlier this year. He'd had it from new, but would I have risked a Skoda 10 years ago – even from someone I knew and trusted? Never! I looked at the JD power surveys and Skoda used to come nowhere.

Skoda had a reputation for being low value and prone to problems. The jokes about them were everywhere:

'Why do Skodas have heated rear windscreens?'[4]

'So you can keep your hands warm when pushing them.'

Then Volkswagen AG (VAG) bought Skoda and set about turning their image around. Using the Golf platform to establish a much higher quality vehicle, they then used innovative advertising to get the repositioning across – and haven't been afraid to poke fun at themselves. They ran a series of ads where their latest model – a very attractive and high quality Fabia – was subjected to accusations of 'not being a Skoda' – because it looked too good!

Everyone laughed, but the proof of the pudding (or in today's advertising terms, 'what's in the cake') was in its performance (and its rapidly rising position in the JD power surveys[5]*).*

Effectively the Skoda is a Golf in a better-value package – the quality message was established to the point where some people in the motor trade now think Skoda is better than VW! They're now top of surveys for reliability.

So we've established that fixing problems creates stronger attachments, so there's nothing wrong with admitting there's problem, it's simply an opportunity to enhance your reputation.

---

[4] More Skoda jokes here http://skoda-jokes.blogspot.co.uk/2008/02/skoda-jokes.html
[5] The JD Power Survey is a form of gossip – they call it an unbiased assessment, but it's still gossip, in the same way Which? Magazine is the opinion of its researchers!

THE POINT OF THIS CHAPTER

So why is reputation important?

Paying attention to your reputation can be the difference between making a profit and losing your business. Potential customers are influenced by your reputation and can decide not to even try to do business with you, without having ever met you or found out what your company is capable of. On the other hand, if you have an unhappy customer, it's worth moving heaven and earth to sort their problems out – they'll bring you more business in the long term.

What you're aiming for is good Reputational Gossip!

A brand for a company is like a reputation for a person. You earn reputation by trying to do hard things well.

JEFF BEZOS

CHAPTER 3

What are people saying?

Wherever you meet people someone's reputation is being enhanced or destroyed – or worse still ignored. Every networking event you go to affects your reputation – and that of other people, that's why we go, to make sure we are not unknown and ignored.

Do you recognise any of these conversations?

A keen networker greets an accountant that has been missing from the networking group for a while.

'Hi there! Where have you been? Haven't seen you for ages.'

'Oh, you know, clients leave everything to the last minute.' (smiles).

Ten minutes later the networker is talking to a new financial advisor: *'I think Tom, the accountant, might be struggling a bit. He seems to be having trouble with some of his clients.'*

Meanwhile another group member is complaining: *'I think I might have to buy a new chair for my desk. My back is killing me.'*

The group leader comes to her aid right away; *'I know exactly who you need to talk to. Sarah is an Ergonomic expert and she is brilliant! She made me sit on an ordinary chair and identified five things that would take the strain off my back right away. She does a free 10-minute review – why don't you talk to her?'*

As you might imagine, the lady with the painful back is very happy to have that initial conversation with such a glowing recommendation.

In another corner of the room a business consultant and a network marketer are having a conversation.

Business consultant: *'Great to see you! This is a really good group, isn't it?'*

Network Marketer: *'Yes, I have several customers already in the group.'*

'Really? Well, that's great. (Thinks: I hope he doesn't try and sell me some kind of cream). It sounds like you're very successful – ah, there's Joe, please excuse me, just need to ask him a question before I forget.'

The business consultant grabs Joe and says: *'Good grief, that network marketer chap is really pushy, isn't he?'*

It's amazing how quickly people make judgments about others – with only the minimum of information on which to base them!

However, people help with problems too. This printer is fortunate to have got into conversation with a really good connector.

Printer: *'I don't know what to do; a client has just given me a brochure to print and it's really rubbish. I don't know whether to say nothing or make a comment and risk upsetting them.'*

The connector: *'That's a shame. Do you know who designed it for them?'*

Printer: *'No, I'm not even sure they've used a designer – and I don't think it's going to market their company very well. It seems such a waste of money to publish something that doesn't do the job.'*

The Connector: *'Why don't you ask them if they need some help with the design and message to ensure the brochure really works hard for them? Fantastic Design are good people and they're quite reasonable, I know several people they've done work for and the feedback is very good – both from a personal and professional perspective. They're very good at ensuring projects have the right focus.'*

Printer: *'That's good to hear. I'd definitely be interested in talking to them.'*

The printer feels much more confident in tackling his client about upgrading their brochure with some back up.

Almost certainly you will have heard or been involved with similar conversations yourself. There's no right or wrong here – only impressions and gossip. However, reputations have been created or destroyed with less!

No smoke without fire

The examples above are typical of a networking event. However, people chat everywhere, in the tea room, in the gaggle of nicotine addicts or by the water cooler inside an organisation; at meetings, conferences and other events outside the organisation. Not to mention social situations where people meet in a pub, bar or coffee shop.

In fact, people chat on train journeys and in public places, to each other and on their mobile phones. It can be impossible not to eavesdrop and it's astonishing how much sensitive information people share without consideration of who can hear. Sometimes it's not difficult to work out who or what they're talking about and, with today's technology in your pocket, it's easy to pass that on to a huge audience via social media.

It's almost impossible to stop people talking about you – you can't be everywhere and you can't predict what will trigger them thinking of and mentioning you.

Even when, as in some of the examples above, the 'facts' are based on assumptions that are not necessarily correct, people will still talk. The speaker may admit that their opinion is based on a feeling instead of facts, but their comments will still be stored away by the people in their conversation.

The piece of information may be disregarded – until the person who heard it hears something else that appears to corroborate it. The additional information may not be about the same issue, but adds to the hearer's impression of the person they're hearing about.

I met a lady in a networking group I attend regularly and she was full of enthusiasm with a lively personality; let's call her Sandy. She had a business supplying business gifts.

There was a point at which we were going to work on a project together and she did lots of research and seemed to be really well-organised and I was quite impressed. As it happens that project didn't happen – nothing to do with Sandy's input – and then shortly after she disappeared off the radar.

Several months later Sandy contacted me and asked me to do some work for her on marketing material for her new business. She already had lots of glowing testimonials and I did the job – with which she was pleased.

A month or two later I was contacted by a mutual business connection asking for a reference for Sandy. I told her what I knew, but was surprised when this contact explained her reservations were based around an article published in a national woman's magazine about Sandy's personal life. I read the article and was surprised – there was nothing too shocking, but I felt it was poor judgment for a business person to reveal her private life in quite that way.

I had recommended Sandy's services to a friend and she asked for a quote. After being let down – twice – over meetings to discuss her needs and provide a quote, she got an e-mail saying that Sandy was 'having to sell' the company.

My impression of Sandy has gone from enthusiastic, fun and well-organised to poor judgment, unreliable and – frankly – flaky.

Who's talking?

It might be easier to work out who isn't! We all talk and most of the time mean no harm by our comments, but if someone mentions a name and you know that person, it's inevitable that you will pay some attention to what's being said.

Your suppliers talk about you – they will certainly complain 'in confidence' to close associates if they are having problems with your account. They may also be a source of reference for others who are thinking of supplying you and want to check out what you're like as a customer. Every business has customers that they wish would find someone else to get products and services from – they are more trouble than they're worth and some brave people sack customers. You really don't want to be one of those.

Your customers talk about you – and that can be really good. After all, we all want advocates and raving fans who love what we do and are happy to tell the rest of the world. You'd better be very sure that your customers are fans and not simply still customers through inertia.

Prospects – people who might become a customer – talk about you during their search for potential suppliers. They're trying to find out what other people think about you, your services (or products) and the way you do business. Most of us are more likely to be persuaded by the opinion of someone we know than a bunch of testimonials from 'unknown' sources. Maybe it's the cynic that says anyone could have written them – and we're too lazy to check them out, so we ask around.

Other business people talk about you and their experience of you. They may have heard about you in several places, they may have seen you do a short presentation at a networking event, they may have read a magazine or newspaper article about you, or they may have found your page on Facebook or seen your tweets on Twitter. They will have an opinion and won't think twice about voicing it if the subject of conversation turns your way.

When people make judgments

Today's world is so full of choices that it doesn't take much to dislodge a customer. The US News and World Report survey says that the reasons customers leave are because:

1%	die.
3%	move away.
5%	develop other friendships – they meet someone they like who delivers the same product or service.
9%	leave for competitive reasons, usually price driven or they get more services for the same price.
14%	are dissatisfied with the product (and often haven't bothered to tell you).
68%	have had a bad experience with someone who works for you!

The most obvious point at which judgment takes place is when someone has experienced your service. This is likely to be most memorable if they've had a bad experience. Frustration, irritation and anger are all like lighter fuel for the tongue. When we have been badly done by we want to moan about it – to anyone who will listen!

When we've received good service – as we said in the last chapter – people don't notice it so much. We expect good service, so for people to talk about it, it needs to be exceptional – beyond what they were expecting.

LESLEY'S STORY

I do a lot of networking – I know it helps my business because I track where my business comes from. However, I can't be everywhere, so I choose to attend specific events I think are the most productive for me.

There's one man who I've met regularly at a couple of groups that I have attended and whom I have done business with. He is definitely one of my fans (and I'm one of his too!) One day he e-mailed me and this is what he said:

'I thought I'd tell you that every time I see someone at a network, two things become obvious:

1. They all know you, or have heard of you.

2. They all like and admire you.

It's nice that I can tell people that you have done work for me in the past and to be able to pass on to you the good vibe as well as feedback that you engender within networking.'

As you might imagine, I glowed for the rest of the day and I still do every time I read it! It's very reassuring to hear that people are saying good things about me.

However, it's not just about being a nice guy; to be the person that gets talked about you need to be memorable.

People remember things that stand out.

A customer service expert called Wendy Evans wrote a book called *How to get new business in 90 days and keep it forever*. It's now out of print, but what stuck in my mind was that she did things that people remembered.

She would go on a 'chocolate tour' and visit her clients and prospective clients with a huge box of chocolates and invite them to try a couple: 'Just popped in to share these with you'.

She also sent people handwritten greetings cards after she had phoned them – these stayed on people's desks for weeks and months. People didn't forget Wendy – and for all the right reasons.

This is a good point for you to stop and think (and maybe jot down some notes).

- What stands out about your service?
- Why do people remember you first – before any of your competitors?

If they don't, then there's something that you can work on right away.

Michael Jackson – innocent and guilty

The late pop star's final few years were fraught with controversy. He was tried for child molestation and *acquitted* by a jury in 2005.

So he was innocent.

However, within days, the jurors had sold their stories to the press and the core message that came over was 'We felt that there was something probably wrong, but there was no proof, and were asked to give a verdict based on the evidence. There wasn't enough evidence to give a guilty verdict.'

So Michael Jackson was **guilty by association** in the world's media[6].

People make judgments based only on hearsay. They may never have done business with you – in fact, in today's world, with the information highway, they may never have even met you.

A reputation in just 140 characters

Even people who don't know you have an opinion about you.

---

[6] Jackson Unveiled – James Fletcher, Jan Disley and Ros Wynne-Jones

If you're active on social media then your Twitter feed, Facebook posts and Linked In comments will all help people to form an opinion of you. If you tweet about taking the dog for a walk and what you had for lunch, their opinion of you will be based on social stuff only; it won't tell them about your business expertise or knowledge base. They may even put you down as a lightweight, simply because of your posts about your personal life. They are missing the point of *social* media, but it's still wise to think before you post anything that may be misinterpreted. It's also good practice to consider which social media platforms and pages you choose for the type of post you're making.[7]

However, if you share tips, advice, point people at interesting and useful blogs and generally appear to know what you're talking about, your social media following will rate you as a knowledgeable professional in your industry.

This means that, if you're smart, you can manage your own reputation to some extent.

How the professionals do it

We all know people who are very good at managing their reputation. Some of the people on your Top 10 list from Chapter 1 are prime examples. Let's look at some of the big hitters, for whom reputation is critical.

Madonna has manipulated her reputation over the years from the blonde vamp in provocative outfits aiming to shock to today's superstar with style, with 'mother' and 'successful businesswoman' firmly embedded in her profile. Some of you will remember the scandalous book, *Sex,* she produced in the early 1990s – getting her banned in some countries. She sold 1.5 million books in a few days and followed it up with an album called *Erotica*, also destined to sell millions.

After a couple of film roles which almost brought her career down, she deliberately set about toning down her image and, with the critical claim that *Evita* brought her, rescued her reputation from the brink.

---

[7] Facebook is social, but a Facebook Page can be used for business, Google+ has a similar process.

She has been acclaimed as a businesswoman, with enterprises including fashion design, writing children's books, and film directing and producing. You only have to see a live Madonna show to know how expert she has become as a manager of her reputation; most people go away thinking just what she wanted them to!

It would be interesting to know whether she rates Elton John's negative comments, published in 2012, as 'good press' or 'damaging'.

Pop stars and actors all know how important reputation is, although some of them actively pursue a bad reputation.

Cliff Richard has always been squeaky clean – although when he came out as a born again Christian some of his fans didn't like it. He has said in interviews that he is very aware that his longevity as a pop icon is due to him actively managing his reputation.

The Rolling Stones – who are of a similar vintage (just a little younger) – although now all well into their 60s – cultivate a very different reputation. They are still seen with beautiful young women (in some cases younger than their sons and daughters) and revel in their bad boy personas.

Look at **Des O'Connor**. The butt of Eric and Ernie's jokes[8] (although they were friends), he was distinctly uncool and the kind of entertainer that everyone's granny liked. Now he's become the elder statesman of the entertainment industry: he has worked with everyone from Buddy Holly to Jason Donovan. Now in his 80s and on his fourth marriage, he became a father again in his 70s, and revived his talk-show skills in the early 2000s with Mel Sykes. He's got respect from everyone because his reputation has changed and evolved.

When a negative becomes a positive

Taking a step away from the stars, reputation management can be just as effective in business – and something that may appear to be a big blot on your reputation can be turned around.

---

[8] One of the funniest Eric, Ernie and Des clips http://www.youtube.com/watch?v=Nqn2lnx9Sbl

PETER'S STORY

It's no secret that I declared bankruptcy not long after our bestseller, And Death Came Third, was published. In fact, it's well documented in my subsequent book, Running on Empty. At the time it was humbling and painful.

The effect it had on my confidence was dramatic, instant and far reaching. My unshakeable belief had disappeared and I didn't know how to get it back.

My family, however, saw it differently and, when the court case was done and the arrangements made they said 'Dad, thank goodness you can move on with your life now. Go do what you're good at!' Through the tough months that followed they never stopped encouraging me and never once complained or criticised.

For a while I believed that I would never run my own business again, but eventually it became clear that this was still the right thing to do – using the lessons I had learned by getting it wrong.

It's interesting that in the USA bankruptcy is seen as simply a battle scar along the route to success and really successful people consider it as part of the process of earning their stripes. In the UK it's a sign of failure and talked of in hushed tones or not at all. A bankrupt is often regarded as 'a bit dodgy'.

I don't see bankruptcy as a rite of passage, but nor do I see it as evidence that someone is not to be trusted. It's all in the way you deal with it. Everyone makes mistakes and hindsight is a wonderful thing. To me the secret is looking at what went wrong and then ensuring that the new business doesn't travel that route again.

The business we launched was Positive Ground and it represents everything we stand for as a family. We choose who we work with, the suppliers that we use and the expertise we offer. We meet regularly to work ON the business keeping it on track and avoiding the pitfalls that we now are only too well aware exist. Of course, we've had our challenges – every business does – but I'm pleased to report that it's growing steadily.

The feedback from being upfront and admitting my failures has been enormously positive. With several people telling me that it's made them see me in a different – positive – light.

THE POINT OF THIS CHAPTER

So what are people saying about you?

What do you say when you meet people that influences their opinions? If you are active online then a plan of action to build and enhance your reputation is essential. Be aware of what people are saying about you and what you can do to influence that positively.

When you have negative experiences what do you do to turn them around and use them to apply for future success?

It's not only how you present yourself, but how you are seen to deal with life's – and business's – ups and downs that affects your reputation and how people see you and speak about you. If you have a team get them involved. In fact, get them to do it for themselves too.

Take a few moments to look back on the ups and downs of your business. What have you learned and how have you used it to influence your reputation?

It takes 20 years to build a reputation and five minutes to ruin it. If you think about that, you'll do things differently.

WARREN BUFFETT

CHAPTER 4

How life has changed

Today we live in a speeded-up world. In our grandparents' day things were much slower. It's said that we access more information in a week than our grandparents did in a lifetime!

The world has changed – and there's no going back.

PETER'S STORY

Everyone in the Midlands knows the Black Country Spine road – but it's only been there for 20 years or so. The area used to be the Midlands industrial heartlands with pressing plants and engineering works. It had been there since the industrial revolution in the 1800s and during the First World War was the home of the munitions industry.

The Brummie and Black Country accents are said to have originated because, in those days, ear defenders had not been invented and the workers, who came from all over the country, north and south and from Ireland, would lose their hearing in the lower range. Their wives had to speak in a higher range to get through and the sing song accent developed.

It was grimy and grubby and it was also where my great grandfather worked. Even as recently as the 1970s it was an industrial area, where the Midlands heavy industry was based, but all that has gone now.

As you drive down the dual carriageway that now carves a path through the middle you can see acres of warehousing and wholesalers, relieved by the occasional shopping complex with all the fast food you could possibly want.

Distribution has taken over from manufacturing. Goods are made in places like China and simply imported, stored and distributed.

There are still jobs in the area, but they're a very different kind of job in today's world.

Of course, there have always been means of information getting from place to place – popularly known as the bush telegraph! In reality, letters, phone, telegrams, telex machines and fax machines.

Remember when you sat down and wrote on a piece of paper with a pen, licked the envelope and the stamp and put it in the post box? If it was urgent and you sent it First Class then you got an answer within a week.

PETER'S STORY

When I was 16, I got a job as a junior clerk for a scaffolding company in Yardley, (a district in Birmingham). This lowly role meant I was responsible for getting the toast for everyone in the morning – until I got promoted to trainee!

I sat three desks away from Olwyn, who was a generously-proportioned lady and the Queen of the comptometer. For those of you who don't know what a comptometer is, it was a mechanical calculator with banks of keys the operator thumped, and it rattled away loudly.

Olwyn's fingers raced across the keys and her skills were much revered.

One day a lady called Elaine came along. Olwyn and Elaine were like chalk and cheese. Elaine was young, blonde and willowy and wore the mini-skirts that were high fashion at the time (early 1970s). She quietly undid her briefcase and took out an electronic calculator and started totting up the invoice figures. The electronic gizmo was not only much smaller and quieter but, with Elaine's fingers flying round the keypad, also much, much faster.

Olwyn's face said it all. She realised that her job had just disappeared from under her nose in the tap of a key. She stayed with the company and became the post room manager, moving on to manage the franking machine.

For me it was something I never forgot. I watched someone lose their job right in front of me because technology had moved on. It has always reminded me that life can change in a nanosecond.

If you're under 20 you probably think we're bonkers, but believe us, even business people would launch wads of post and then wait patiently for replies. Today we're checking our e-mail many times a day wondering why someone has not replied yet. In fact, you can have a whole conversation by e-mail in the space of a few minutes. From the advent of the BlackBerry, this has been possible anywhere, any time and spawned the phrase 'Crackberry' – people are now addicted to their smartphones.

Today's kids don't spend their time with the Encyclopaedia Britannica to hand when they do their school projects. They get on Wikipedia and Google and everything they need is there at the touch of a few keys.

Gone are the days when information not available at home required an expedition to the library. Today's libraries have computers available for you to access the internet too.

There have always been ways to get information from A to B (and sometimes to all the other letters in the alphabet too) – it's just that the advent of the internet and computers in most people's homes has extended the speed of information travelling from place to place.

PETER'S STORY

When I was a sales person I would phone the office from a telephone box first thing in the morning and last thing in the afternoon using a pile of 10p pieces. They didn't expect to hear from me during the day and they had no means of contacting me until I phoned in again. I did my own thing; everyone was happy and I was fairly chilled.

The minute they put a phone in the car everything changed.

My first car phone was the size of a brick and not something I wanted to drag around with me. It was a work tool and it would be rare that I might think of using it for non-work calls, without it being a real emergency. However, it did mean that the office could get hold of me – no matter where I was.

I have to admit that I did use it to order pizza from the takeaway in Stafford, where we used to live. They always knew it was me because I was the only one of their customers with a mobile phone. It was that much of novelty back in 1990.

The outcome of being in constant contact for me was that 'chilled' became a thing of the past and the word 'stressed' was a better description of how I felt at work.

Phones got smaller and more portable. It was only a few years ago that everyone had a Nokia 6210 (you can still get them if you want a phone that just makes calls and sends texts) and they swept through the mobile phone market, carving out a huge chunk of the sales. Then the BlackBerry changed how we used the phone with its ability to process e-mail. The iPhone gave us 24/7 communication e-mail, online access, chat and apps; it's almost impossible to move without a phone firmly welded to your fist.

With computing power escalating so that your smartphone has a memory many times that of a desktop computer even 10 years ago, it means that information has become completely portable. The only thing that stops you getting what you want when you want is the lack of a signal. If you see anyone doing strange things in the street, waving their phones about, it's usually because they can't get the signal they need to update their Facebook status.

It's how the world evolves. There was a time, not all that long ago, when we watched films with a Betamax tape machine, then the VCR pushed it out of the marketplace, only to be usurped by DVDs and BluRay discs.

The iPod killed minidiscs; CDs pushed out cassette tapes (and who remembers having an eight-track in their car?) MP3s replaced CDs and now the music is all 'up there' in The Cloud.

Marketing is everything

Dell brought out a gadget that was very similar to the iPad, around the same time as Apple. However, they didn't see the potential, didn't market it well and shelved it. Apple are innovators, Dell are box-shifters and couldn't see how it would catch the imagination of people. Their take was 'it won't change anything', but, as we all know, the iPad has changed everything, both business-wise and personally.

The techno-corporates have coined the phrase 'device agnostic[9]' to indicate that they have no preference for whether their employees

---

[9] The literal meaning of 'agnostic' is 'being unable to decide' or 'uncommitted, but accurate interpretation has never stopped the technological world coining a new meaning!

use their own devices – smart phones, iPads and laptops – or the company's. That shows just how prevalent personal technology is today – most business people are expected to have these devices.

It's information overload and, to my mind, like trying to play pool with everyone else trying to play at the same time.

Everyone is getting so much information that their attention spans are getting shorter and people complain of poor memories. It's not so much not being able to remember as having so much to remember – no wonder people sometimes feel that their brains are full!

The internet and social media has also extended everyone's reach. Everything is linked together on a multitude of platforms and types of social media. What one person says on Facebook is reported on Twitter, picked up on someone else's LinkedIn feed and in no time the whole world is talking about it.

When *And Death Came Third* was launched in April 2006, Facebook was only a year old and it became a best seller with no social media. The whole PR campaign was done by e-mail with the commitment of many friends who used their newsletters to spread the word in true referral style. This was only six years ago; today the idea of launching *The Reputation Game* without using social media or other online marketing media is unthinkable.

The information highway

The early social media platforms started in the 1990s and Ecademy launched in the UK in 1998 with LinkedIn following in 2002. Little did people realise what was coming.

MySpace was launched in 2003, but was rapidly usurped by Facebook, which appeared in 2004. Twitter came along in 2006 – although people are surprised at how long it's been around.

There are now hundreds of social media platforms. Facebook and YouTube are visited nearly as often as Google – which is a search engine. People are using social media as means of finding information.

Because our office is in a library complex, it's very peaceful – until 4pm when the kids arrive on their little silver scooters to use the four computers. In no time they're on the internet. Are they researching their homework projects on Google? Not always, some of them are playing games, but, when they want to know something they go to YouTube.

This was demonstrated even more when a business colleague was bemoaning the fact that her son would come home and sit down at the computer and surf YouTube. She pointed out that he was supposed to be doing his homework and suggested he got on Google and start doing his research.

His response was 'I don't use Google. If there isn't a video about it, then it probably isn't worth knowing.' He used YouTube as a search engine.

In fact, news is now breaking on social networks and the influence of the traditional news media has become secondary. Today we don't have to be consumers only – we don't have to have the ear of a friendly journalist to get our views out to a massive audience. We just need a smartphone.

There is no longer any need to rely on what the press say. If people involved in a story want to have their say, they can – publicly, nationally and internationally.

A good story will go global – fast.

A bad story will go global – faster!

In the UK, Susan Boyle appeared to be a frumpy, middle-aged Scottish lady and everyone expected her to be one of the freaks on the show *Britain's Got Talent,* especially after her painful introduction where she tried to flirt with Simon Cowell. However, the moment she started to sing everyone sat up and took notice. She had a fantastic voice. That, in itself, was not unusual – that's what the show is all about. However, the YouTube video of her audition and the panel's astonished faces went viral in days, with people e-mailing each other to watch the clip. It had millions of hits in the week following her performance. She has gone on to become a singing superstar worldwide.

Wikipedia gives several examples of how local stories have gained international attention through the use of social media.

- News media coverage of the Trayvon Martin shooting in Sanford, Florida was minimal until social media users made the story recognisable through their constant discussion of the case. Approximately one month after the fatal shooting of Trayvon Martin, its online coverage by everyday Americans garnered national attention from mainstream media journalists.

- Social Media was also influential in the widespread attention given to the revolutionary outbreaks in the Middle East and North Africa during 2011.

- The ongoing Kony 2012 campaign surfaced first on YouTube and later garnered a great amount of attention from mainstream news media journalists, who now monitor social media sites to inform their reports on the movement.

People talk to each other on social media and – because of the public nature of most conversations – the world listens.

PETER'S STORY

In November 2011, there was a flash mob on the 19.57 train heading out of Euston. A man started singing Lovely Day, then gradually other people joined in until there was a choir singing in beautiful harmony.

In the carriage were a young couple and the girl dug the boy in the ribs and said 'It's a flash mob, quick get your phone out.'

He fumbled in his pocket and just as he withdrew his hand the singing stopped. He sank to one knee and presented his girlfriend with the little box that contained an engagement ring and asked her to marry him.

The choir then continued singing.

How do I know about this? Well, I know because my daughter-in-law, Emily, was part of the choir (as was the young man who carried out the proposal) and she sent us the link to the YouTube video, which was loaded so that the couple's friends and family could see it.

Then Sara-Beth, my daughter, came into the office and we said 'You've got to watch this.'

After a couple of seconds she said 'I've already seen it. That's going the rounds, I picked it up on social media and all my friends are talking about it.' She had no idea that Emily was in it (we had to point her out), but had already e-mailed several friends with the link, just because it was a great video.

It went viral and the couple appeared on national TV in the UK and even Good Morning America in the States.

This phenomenon is not confined to the young – the demographics of Facebook users shows well over a third of them are over 35; with 8% of those over 55. It's a great way for people to keep in touch with family no matter how far away they live.

So information is available to people of all ages and it's right under their nose when they go online to talk to their friends.

In fact, when it's their friends talking, they are much more likely to take it seriously.

Social media – make or break

Unless you are a hermit living in a cave and nobody knows that you exist, your reputation is at the mercy of the internet. You could be talked about anywhere – on any social media network, via phone, text, messaging service, instant chat on Skype, MSN or ICQ – the possibilities are endless.

You can't stop people talking – you just need to hope that it's all positive. This means that you need to be conscious of what you say and what you do. Unlike some silly celebrities who tweet whatever comes into their heads and within hours their unguarded comments have become international news stories.

Ashton Kutcher (a well-known actor and avid tweeter) – with millions of followers – posted an ill-advised tweet about Penn State coach, Joe Paterno, which caused such an uproar that he announced that he was handing over his Twitter account to his managers (he's back in control now though). Oh yes, he also posted a picture of, his ex-wife, Demi Moore's bottom taken whilst ironing in a white bikini with a far from appropriate comment.

Lily Allen (singer and daughter of actor Keith Allen) complained on Twitter that the death of Osama Bin Laden was taking the spotlight off the fact that it was her 26th birthday. Even though her tongue was probably firmly in her cheek, it didn't exactly count as positive PR.

Courtney Love (singer, songwriter and actress) was sued by a fashion designer who alleged that she attempted a smear campaign against her on Twitter.

Business people don't always get it right either:

The media savvy people who work at Mars-owned Skittles, instead of building their own website, redirected Skittles.com to a Twitter search results page. They were not prepared for the flood of prank posts such as: 'Skittles got stuck in my mouth while I was driving, forced me to slam into orphanage, killing hundreds. I'll never eat them again.'

It's wise to think carefully before posting – which is what the young lady who had just landed a well-paid job from internet company Cisco should have done. She tweeted the following:

> *Cisco just offered me a job! Now I have to weigh the utility of a fatty paycheck against the daily commute to San Jose and hating the work.*

> Soon after, the company rescinded the offer, tweeting: *Who is the hiring manager? I'm sure they would love to know you will hate the work. We here at Cisco are versed in the web.*[10]

It isn't even as if you can practise damage control – you can't possibly see what everyone says about you and your company. In fact, if you could afford to, you could employ someone full time and they'd still miss some of the comments made about you.

It only takes one comment and you're damned. It doesn't matter whether it's true or not – you can't delete it. If it's got your name on it and someone puts your name in a search engine there's a chance that it will appear.

---

[10] More details of these and other celebrity gaffes can be found here
http://www.cleo.com.au/the-worst-celebrity-twitter-gaffes.htm; and here
http://www.telegraph.co.uk/technology/twitter/5250680/Top-10-worst-tweets.html and here
http://www.huffingtonpost.com/2011/04/04/worst-twitter-pr-fails_n_844748.html#s=263338

Your digital footprint is indelible. It's there forever.

There are people who specialise in reputation reclamation. Their strategy is usually to flood the internet with positive information about you in the hope that it will push negative things down the rankings to the point where they are so far down that nobody will bother looking that far down.

LESLEY'S STORY

I was giving a lecture to a group of students on website readability and the issue of social media came up. I asked them how many of them had a Facebook account – all of them had.

Their course was in Equine Studies, but they would shortly be looking for a job with stables or horse trainers or launching their own business.

I asked them if anybody had photos or comments on their Facebook profiles that they would prefer potential employers or clients did not see. A certain amount of giggling was followed by some embarrassed looks.

One of them said 'But I wouldn't let a potential employer see my Facebook account.'

'How many people have you accepted as 'friends' that you don't really know?' I asked.

Everyone exchanged looks. It was clear that almost no one had even considered this.

You never know who might be able to look at your profile – make sure you don't put anything on it you wouldn't mind your future boss, or your best client, seeing. Sometimes it can be difficult when other people tag you in a photo – however, you can remove those tags and you can set your privacy settings so that they can't tag you.

There is the other side of the coin. The 'make' side of social media.

It's a very powerful tool to build a positive image and enhance your reputation simply by being visible and sharing your knowledge freely.

If you're seen as an authority on your specialist subject it will create a positive reputation over time and more and more people will discover your expertise. It takes a little effort, but is worth it to create a high profile that generates respect.

Good examples are the ubiquitous Stephen Fry, journalist and broadcaster, Richard Madeley and our own good friend, Alan Stevens, who is well known in speaking, training and media circles and has a brilliant reputation in those areas.

The curse of e-mail

It's true that some of the under 25s have stopped using e-mail and carry out all their communication via Facebook and Twitter. However, despite the alternative means of communication, e-mail remains a must for businesses, but it's important to be forever mindful of how you manage this. We all get spam and if you become known as a spammer your reputation will take a dive.

Only 20% of e-mail is not spam – at least our spam filter catches between 79-81% of incoming mail month in, month out. Typically most of us only read about 20% of the e-mail that makes it to the inbox. That means that only FIVE e-mails out of every hundred are read. Most of us read emails from people we know and those with subject lines that make some kind of impact – otherwise delete, delete, delete.

I know people who work in large organisations who claim that some days it takes them until lunchtime to answer their e-mail. That's a really worrying thought!

With today's mobile media it can be much easier to get a response from someone by dropping them an e-mail than by ringing them up and leaving a voice mail. However, that doesn't mean you should abuse the medium!

THE POINT OF THIS CHAPTER

So why is today's world different when it comes to your reputation?

Information travels so far and so fast in such a short time that it's possible for someone in Indonesia to read about your latest business contract seconds after its been posted.

Being careful of what you type in social media platforms will help to protect your reputation – so think twice before you type, you don't know who will see it or pass it on.

Online chat can influence the news – whilst that can be good, it can also be disastrous if it's not the news that you want broadcast.

Even good old e-mail can influence how people see you – be a thoughtful e-mailer.

If you write a letter electronically, you can't destroy it later. It's there for posterity and it all contributes to your reputation.

A reputation once broken may possibly be repaired,
but the world will always keep their eyes on
the spot where the crack was.

JOSEPH HALL

CHAPTER 5

Establishing your reputation

You can't stop people talking – and writing – about you and your business. However, you can influence what they say. The first rule of managing your reputation is to know yourself.

This chapter will look at your brand, your image, the actions you take, what you say and what people know about you – and you can influence all of this.

Your brand

There are two sides to your brand. There's your personal brand and the marketing brand of your business.

If you're a small business or sole proprietor it's almost certain that you *are* your brand. If you own or run a larger organisation the whole company will have its own brand. However, that doesn't mean that you don't still need a personal brand – after all, people buy people.

There are plenty of people who can help you to develop a personal brand. Lesley Everett has written a book about it[11] and works with people from speakers to corporate executives on getting their brand to be consistent and authentic.

There are plenty of people around who consult on personal branding. We've both done this at different times and Peter learned to wear two button jackets, the colours that suited him best (and the ones that didn't!) complementary shirts and ties. He has saved a fortune long term and got a much better result.

---

[11] Walking Tall: Key Steps to Total Image Impact

Lesley changed her colour schemes and got lots of compliments. Strangely, nobody knew what it was that had changed – the most popular guesses were 'new hairdo', 'lost weight', but actually, she just stopped wearing black and started wearing colours that made her look much better!

People who really know about personal branding and use it effectively are often celebrities. For instance:

- Gok Wan – known for making people feel good about themselves regardless of their shape or size.
- Jamie Oliver – a chap-next-door image, and passionate about school dinners, young people learning to cook and no-nonsense cooking.
- Michael McIntyre – a bouncy comic who skips round the stage and is always slightly astonished at the things people do.

We all recognise them and that's what you're aiming for – a recognisable brand.

So what creates a brand?

Your personal brand is developed around your values and beliefs. It's what you stand for and what people buy about you, as an individual.

If you ask most people what their core values are, they can, with a bit of prompting, come up with about 20 words to describe their strong values. This might include words and phrases like:

- Enthusiastic
- Problem solver
- Getting things done
- Practical approach
- Making customers happy
- Having fun

A good exercise is to get someone to ask you the question 'What's really important to you about your business?' and then they write down everything you say. This leaves you free to let your mind work, without interrupting it with the writing process.

When you run out of ideas, they should ask you the same question again. This usually opens up a few more possibilities.

If you do this three or four times you'll have pretty much all your core values in a list.

It's now a matter of ranking them. A neat way to do this is to write each value on a sticky note and then starting with any one, take a second one and decide if it is more or less important than the starting one. Continuing this process will give you a ranked order with all the sticky notes in order of importance.

It's impossible to pay attention to 20 different values all the time. Take the top four or five and stay focused on them.

Peter's top five are:

- Family.
- Love.
- Honesty.
- Fun.
- Caring.

The five are not in order because they move around due to different situations if Peter had to choose his top one it would always be family

Lesley's top five are:

- Independence.
- Loving my work.
- Consistent high quality results.
- Recognition as an expert in my field.
- Being around positive people.

However, some things mean different things to different people. During a workshop two people had 'independence' as their top value, but on closer examination, their interpretation of that was vastly different. One meant 'not having someone else telling me what to do'; the other meant 'being able to afford to live the life I want with my partner'.

It doesn't matter – they're your values – as long as you know what they mean and your business fits with them.

Where do values come from?

Generally they are developed during your formative years, influenced by your upbringing and the people around you. They don't change much over the years as a rule and you run your life by them. They are fundamental to who you are and influence how others see you.

We quickly assess if someone's values are similar to our own. Whilst it's unlikely that you will find lots of people with identical values to you, you will need to have some overlap in values to feel comfortable with people.

If you're working in an organisation that has very different values to your own, you will almost certainly be unhappy.

Where there is a big disparity between the values of people who work together it creates discomfort and conflict. You'll find people constantly locking horns. If you've ever worked somewhere and when one individual has left it felt as though a cloud has lifted, you'll know what it means.

Where there is some congruency, we mostly live with the differences and focus on the similarities.

Your personal brand

If you've ever been to a networking meeting you'll see personal branding at work.

First impressions are formed:

- **Personal brand part 1:** People look you up and down and make an assessment based on how you dress, what you smell like, how you greet them, speak to them, whether you're smiling or serious, etc. It takes less than 90 seconds; women make quicker judgments than men (and are usually more accurate).

- **Personal brand part 2:** This is demonstrated by the actions you take, what your value sets are. This will take longer, but if you take a group of people who know you well and ask them to come up with half a dozen words that describe you, the words that each of them suggest will be similar. They've got to know you, watched you operate and made their judgments – and they're rarely far out.

This is what your initial reputation is based upon.

How people see you

Your image is based on many things – what you wear, how you do your hair, what kind of accessories you carry or wear, the car your drive, the house you live in, the place you work, the way in which you present yourself at meetings, the list goes on and on.

When it comes to clothes there's no longer a single right way to dress for business. Quite apart from it depending on the business you're in, 'acceptable' has now stretched way beyond 'suited and booted'.

There's the electrician who wears a suit and tie to networking events and the national business owner who always turns up in jeans and a T-shirt. It seems anything goes.

Fashion does have some impact and new generations will always want to dress differently, act differently, do everything differently from the ones that have gone before (until they realise that it's all been done before!)

20-something men are being seen more and more frequently wearing not only a three-piece suit with a tie – but also with a handkerchief displayed in the breast pocket. Peter was wearing these in the mid-eighties!

Generation X men have gone through the struggle with dressing down and tend to wear suits with no tie or a shirt and jacket with jeans.

Peter admits that he mostly wears a jacket, trousers and open necked shirt these days, but was brought up to be a suit and tie man in business – even if he actually feels most comfortable in jeans and a T-shirt.

Whilst T-shirt and jeans are, in many cases, acceptable, it doesn't work for all age groups. There's always that mutton dressed as lamb image and a vague feeling that people are trying too hard to be hip (now there's a word that dates us).

Women have always had more flexibility and fashion has dictated what is OK – if power suits are in, then turning up in a floaty summer dress and little shrug will have an impact on your image. Very short skirts and very low necklines in business environments will affect your image – even if they are fashionable.

LESLEY'S STORY

I used to work in Dubai in a big organisation and the boss had a very strict dress code for those staff who did not wear uniforms (managers). The men were expected to wear a suit or smart trousers and jacket, a long-sleeved shirt, a tie and a belt on their trousers.

Women were to wear skirts or dresses of a sensible length (no trousers or culottes), tights – regardless of the temperature – and modest necklines.

This wasn't written down anywhere – but when new managers joined the company the message got through quickly.

These values about image rubbed off when we were assessing suppliers. One lady came in who was in the recruitment business. She was very successful and had a thriving business and was looking to get the contract to supply us with staff. As we were a growing organisation already with well over 300 staff, it was a good contract for her to get.

She came to the meeting in a tight, short skirt and a top that, to put it mildly, had all her assets on display. Lots of make-up, tumbling curls and plenty of what, in today's language, we would call 'bling', completed the picture.

She met with two of us, both women, and we both came to the same conclusion; unprofessional – and really didn't understand our company ethos at all. She didn't get the contract.

Accessories all play a part – for women it's the handbag or briefcase or both conundrum and whether that's a neat little thing or a huge rucksack full of stuff. Is it a designer label or something cheaper and more practical?

However, it's also jewellery; like the lady above, too much doesn't shout 'success', it often screams 'tasteless'. Accessories should enhance, not be the primary focus.

For men, it's the watch. You can spend thousands on a watch and, even in today's world where the time is displayed on your phone, laptop, car dashboard, everywhere, the watch is a symbol of your status. It doesn't have to be a gold Rolex, but it does have to be classy.

The car you drive also adds to (or detracts from) your image.

PETER'S STORY

A few years ago our accountant bought one of those big pick-ups. Out in the country that wasn't all that unusual and I can certainly attest to the fact that it went really well.

Our accountant was then in his late twenties and it was great for his age group and personal style – but, before long he replaced it.

I'd had fun riding in it with him and asked why.

'It doesn't fit the image of an accountant, it made people a bit suspicious of me,' he explained. He's now driving a BMW, which, it seems, calms his clients' nerves.

FOOTNOTE FROM LESLEY

I brought my Camaro Z28 back from Dubai and it stood out like a sore thumb in this country. People couldn't make their minds up about it. Some people said it made me appear successful; others said it made people think I would be too expensive.

Image is 101 things, conscious and unconscious. Be aware that people want to put you in a pigeon hole whether you want it or not. How you present yourself makes a difference and never forget that image change is influenced by mindset. Image is about inside as well as outside.

Actions speak louder than words

Everything that you do helps people to form their opinion of you. You demonstrate personal brand in action in positive or negative way.

For instance, if you meet someone at a networking event and promise to connect them with someone, and then forget to do it, it may not be a big thing, but will contribute to their perception of who you are.

PETER'S STORY

I've just spent a day at a big event in London where a number of experts were presenting their expertise from the platform. Every one of them had a product that they were selling and did a great sales pitch from the platform. The trouble was that, instead of giving me something of value that I could take away with me and put into practice, most of them were totally geared towards flogging me something at £1,997.

One speaker's message was heavily focused on how great it would be to work with him and how important it was to him that he worked with people in a caring and supportive environment. However, his actions demonstrated that his primary focus was how much people were willing to put on their credit cards.

Whilst I appreciate that we all have to make a living, I felt that most of the speakers were there for themselves first and for the audience second.

Every action you take supports your values and congruency needs to be maintained if you don't want people to feel uncomfortable around you.

High value is caring: Peter's wife, Anny, demonstrates it daily. She doesn't have to think about it, it's just what she does. It's hardly surprising that she's been running a company supplying lingerie and swimwear to ladies who have suffered from breast cancer and has continued to do this regardless of the struggles that the family have experienced. Her value of caring comes before everything else.

Every little word

Once people realise the impact of their actions on their existing and potential customers, it's a logical step to see that everything that you say also has an impact. The two go together.

This doesn't mean that you have to go around boasting about your amazing products and services (in fact, please don't), but it is important to discover whether people may be interested in your products and services before trying to make a pitch.

This is where asking good questions is essential. You need to find out what is important to the person with whom you are in conversation, so the focus is on them, not on you. People warm to you much more when you talk about *them*, than when you talk about yourself (which often makes them glaze over).

LESLEY'S STORY

I used to run the customer support and best practice service for Ecademy, one of the earlier social media platforms (launched in 1998). My team worked on a rota responding to people's questions and complaints. There were lots of 'how do I do …' questions and we were always happy to help people use the platform better. However, one of the most frequent complaints was:

I've received a spam message from X. How can I block them?

This was mostly someone who hadn't understood how online networking worked and instead of trying to open a conversation and get to know someone, had a cut-and-paste sales pitch message that they were sending out to as many other members as they could.

Our message to the guilty party used to go something like this:

'We have been informed that you have been contacting members with a sales-style message as your first contact. This tends to upset people as they feel that you are not interested in getting to know them, but just want to sell your products or services.

'If you were at a face-to-face networking event you would be unlikely to grab the first person you bumped into and say "Hello, I sell this product, this is my pitch, do you want to buy it?" without first having a conversation and trying to find out if they had a need or interest.

'Online networking works in the same way. A great way to open the conversation is to read someone's profile and then comment on something that interests you or find something you have in common.

'We hope that this helps you to get more from your membership of Ecademy.'

Nine times out of 10 we received an apology from the member concerned and thanks for helping them to use the platform better.

> *However, I still find that people on other platforms like LinkedIn do the same thing. The first contact I get is a sales message – often from someone who knows nothing about me except that I am in the membership of a group that they are also in. As you can imagine my feelings about them are not warm ones.*

This very concept is why Facebook has been so successful. It's an informal environment where people get to know each other by chatting. People's values are soon revealed when you read the posts on their wall.

THE POINT OF THIS CHAPTER
There's a lot to think about

You do all of this regardless of whether you think about it or not. The secret is to do it more consciously and to present yourself with purpose. The first step in this process is for you to have a clear idea about your own brand, what you stand for and what your standards are.

Think about how others perceive you and your company. Consider how you appear to them in your personal image and also your company brand; it's essential that you present yourself and your organisation consistently in everything you do.

Get into the habit of keeping promises and taking action on the things that are important to you and resonate with your values.

Open your mouth and purse cautiously,
and your stock of wealth and reputation shall,
at least in repute, be great.

JOHN ZIMMERMAN

CHAPTER 6

Taking control of your reputation

Once you're clear about your personal brand and values, as well as your organisation's brand and values, it's time to start being proactive.

You are influencing people all the time, every time you answer the phone, send an e-mail, post on social media, attend network meetings, meet business associates for coffee or new clients to discuss how you might help them. What else could you do to develop your reputation positively?

Actions and your business reputation

In the big, wide business world, long term relationships are based on value sets. That's why Positive Ground[12] works with people they choose to, not just anyone who is willing to pay for services. This makes a big difference to the people within the company as well as the perception of the company from people outside it.

People who don't share the values of the organisation they work for can make customers or clients feel very uncomfortable. If your organisation has a reputation for great service, it only takes one customer-facing employee having a bad day and being rude or off-hand with a customer to ruin your reputation.

Values are in action 24/7 – you don't need to put them in a frame on a wall. Companies with really strong values don't need to tell people what they are; they're demonstrated daily by everything they do and say.

---

[12] http://www.positiveground.co.uk

Putting your values on the wall at best can be overwhelming for the staff to live up to; at worst it will just become wallpaper.

PETER'S STORY

I recently visited a client and as I parked the car I could see through the window of the adjacent office. It was an open plan area with large whiteboards on the walls and each one had 'Rules to adhere to – values in action'. The current batch was numbered 50 to 60!

I'd be astonished if the staff could remember the first 50, let alone the latest batch. Not only overwhelming, but asking people to achieve an almost impossible task.

Having worked with PTI Worldwide[13] in the past I know how well Values in Action really work. Royston Guest, CEO of PTI has built a business based upon the principle of values in action. This is simple, effective and, most of all, transferable to their many clients. When Royston took over PTI (from Peter Thomson) the values were preserved. These are embedded in the organisation's ethos; it's what it does, not a list of rules.

For instance, when big organisations support a cause or charity, it says volumes about their ethics and their concern for others. That's why so many organisations have embraced corporate citizenship and now work with their local communities to improve conditions and facilities.

Ford Motor Company not only has a Charity Committee, but is active in local schools helping young people to understand engineering and providing some of the tools for them to do so.

For many years every employee was paid for two days each year to spend working on a local cause and whole teams went to work building scout huts, gardens in public areas, school facilities and other things that helped the local community.

Needless to say, this has influenced the local community's view of Ford as an employer and engineering as a career. They've also had a good bit of positive press coverage as a result.

Sometimes it's what you don't say that really counts. Some people don't talk a good game, but the actions they take say it all.

---

[13] http://www.pti-worldwide.com

What you say about yourself

This is usually called Marketing! However, a successful marketing campaign will only be successful if your reputation supports what you're saying.

Having said that, what you say about yourself and your company, and the way in which you say it, has a big influence on people's perception of you.

If you stand up at a networking meeting and tell people what you do or a bit about your products then most people accept that, but don't engage particularly well. Our friend and colleague, Andy Lopata,[14] used to be a director of a UK networking organisation and we really like the way he suggested people developed their 60 seconds presentation.

It went something like this:

My name is .... and my company is ....

You know how people have a problem with [insert a common problem that your typical client's experience], well, what we do is [explain the actions that you would take] and [more actions] so that they don't [outline the pain that they currently experience] and that means that they [what the benefit would be for the client].

Finish with name, company and the memory hook – a saying or strapline that people associate with you.

PETER'S STORY

I use a formula called 'problem, pain, solution, result' and I've found it works really well and fits around this structure (which I've been using since God was a boy!) This story demonstrates how effective it can be.

Back in the early days of my sales consultancy I had a client who ran a reprographics company. For those who aren't sure what reprographics actually is, a simple example would be that it is that it's the bit that looks at the design and the packaging of a product and ensures that they work together to produce a robust and attractive package.

---

[14] http://www.lopata.co.uk

The client was another Peter and a bit of a lad, a straight-talking guy who was very good at chatting to the lads on the golf course and his business did very well with his approach. However, he was a bit agitated when he called and wanted me to come to see him the next day – he said it was 'really urgent'.

He was a good client and we had a strong relationship so I made the time to answer his call for help. I arrived and we sat down.

'What's the problem?' I asked.

'Well,' he started, 'in the last six months life has really changed. I know these e-auctions are having an impact on our trade, but that's not the really big problem. My big clients all seem to have invented a new role: purchasing managers. They're buying reprographics one day and chairs the next – and they really don't understand the difference between a product and a service.'

He paused and scratched his head. 'There's another big problem – they're women!'

I laughed – Peter had never had any problem chatting up women – but he wasn't smiling.

'It's all right for you,' he said, 'but I've never sold to women. My style is based more on banter with the blokes and from the moment I start a conversation with one of these purchasing manager women I know I'm blowing it.'

I realised that he was right – he did have a problem and that he needed something to help him through the process of selling to a new type of customer. We went to work and this is what his new – and very successful – approach became:

You know that every Christmas there's a toy that every child desperately wants. It goes in phases and this year's 'must have' will be out of fashion by next year – but that doesn't mean that every parent isn't going to go out and do their best to get little Johnny that special toy.

One year the essential toy was a model Santa and his sleigh with all the reindeer. As with every other family this particular Dad went to Toys4Them and queued with all the other Dads to get the Santa toy for little Johnny. He took it home, Mum wrapped it up in sparkly paper and put it under the tree.

On Christmas morning there it was all ready for little Johnny and he was off-the-scale excited as he ripped off the paper and saw what was inside. That is, until the family realised that Santa had some damage – and so did some of the reindeer – and, you know how lots of Christmas gifts have a game on the packaging? Well, that was damaged too, the packaging hadn't done its job.

Instead of nursing his hangover on Boxing Day morning, Dad was down at Toys4Them – to find that he wasn't alone; all the other Dads were there too, demanding their money back or a replacement.

I can't name the company (or the real name of the toy) – you would know who it was – but this is a real story and it cost the manufacturer millions.

In this case reprographics is a dedicated process to ensure design becomes manageable reality in production – the design idea isn't lost, but it becomes a practical and saleable product. When a new car is launched there is a pre-production model after the design studio stage, but before the production model. The same process is used to deliver an idea into a deliverable reality.

If they had the right reprographics people I wouldn't have this story to tell. I can tell you that we don't have any horror stories like that to tell you about our clients!

So if you want to convert your packaging and design into reality, we can help you.

Lesley's networking breakfast approach varies – this is one based on the formula:

Good morning! I'm Lesley Morrissey from Inside News, I help busy entrepreneurs to plan, protect and promote their reputations.

You know how hard it can be to run a company and ensure your reputation is highly visible and you are seen as a leader in your field?

Well, what we do is work with people who want to create a strategy and structure that will create a compelling message and present it in the places where their target audience is looking.

This means that they build a reputation for their core expertise and demonstrate their knowledge and authority so they become the 'go to' person for their specialism.

I'm Lesley Morrissey from Inside News and I help busy entrepreneurs to get known as the experts in their fields.

Part of my business is writing copy for websites, so I look at a lot of websites that have copy already and are being revamped.

I wish I had a pound for every website I've visited that starts with 'We are a ....' and then every paragraph that follows starts with either 'We', the company name or, sometimes, 'Our'.

This tells me that the company are somewhat self-absorbed and haven't really thought about their reader at all.

I believe that when we talk about ourselves in business, most people are, at best, only politely interested. When we talk about them they start seeing themselves in the situation we are describing.

For instance, 'We help our clients to get a better return on their investments', becomes 'You'll find your money grows quicker and your nest egg will go a lot further.'

Anyone reading that who is planning to make an investment, perhaps, to have a more comfortable retirement, will immediately run that little film in their head of themselves being able to afford whatever it is they have been daydreaming about.

The minute you say 'you', people start relating to what you're saying and it shows that you are interested in your client and their challenges and issues, rather than in what you do.

Sharing your knowledge

One of the most successful strategies for getting a band of fans on board is to give away what you know. Peter talked about this in *Running on Empty* and Lesley has a Treasure Chest[15] on the Lesleywriter website where people can download useful How to documents for free.

Social media is a perfect platform for doing this: share your tips and advice, share useful articles and blogs that you read, connect people with others who do the same. It all helps your visibility and your image.

There are so many people talking on social media that if you're not saying anything it's easy for even your close followers to forget you're there. Sharing your knowledge is an easy and effective way to build

[15] http://www.lesleywriter.com/the-treasure-chest/
[16] http://www.peterthomson.com

both your reputation as someone who 'knows stuff' and raise your profile into the spotlight.

The Magic Matrix

Coincidentally, both of us met Peter Thomson[16] in the 1990s, before we met each other. Peter met him in the early 90s; Lesley towards the end of the decade. So we both know about Peter T's Magic Matrix – sometimes called Windows of Opportunity.

Everyone who discovered it liked it, not least because it reminded people of playing *Battleships*!

If you don't remember *Battleships*, Wikipedia gives this description:

> *The game is played on four grids, two for each player. The grids are typically square – usually 10×10 – and the individual squares in the grid are identified by letter and number. On one grid the player arranges ships and records the shots by the opponent. On the other grid the player records his/her own shots.*
>
> *Before play begins, each player secretly arranges their ships on their primary grid. Each ship occupies a number of consecutive squares on the grid, arranged either horizontally or vertically. The number of squares for each ship is determined by the type of the ship. The ships cannot overlap (i.e., only one ship can occupy any given square in the grid). The types and numbers of ships allowed are the same for each player. These may vary depending on the rules.*

So the playing grid starts like this:

A	B	C	D	E	F	G	H	I	J
1									
2									
3									
4									
5									
6									
7									
8									
9									
10									

Then each player marks the squares occupied by a specified number of aircraft carriers, submarines, battleships, cruisers and destroyers on their own chart.

After the ships have been positioned, the game proceeds in a series of rounds. In each round, each player's turn consists of announcing a target square (e.g. E8) in the opponent's grid which is to be shot at. If a ship occupies the square, then it takes a hit. The player's opponent announces whether or not the shot has hit one of the opponent's ships; the opponent then fires a shot at the first player's ships. When all of the squares of a ship have been hit, the ship is sunk. After all of one player's ships have been sunk, the game ends and the other player wins.

Peter T's Magic Matrix applied this to company's products and services. He would ask people to write down the left hand column all the products and services they offered. You would think that every company knew this, but they don't.

If you don't believe us, you try it.

Products and service

Products and services	A	B	C	D	E	F	G	H	I	J
1										
2										
3										
4										
5										
6										
7										
8										
9										
10										

If you've got more than ten products or services then that's brilliant. Peter has worked with clients who had **thousands!**

In our experience, some of your clients will remember things you've forgotten.

The next step is to enter your Top 10 clients across the top. Then put a cross in every square where that client has experienced that service. All the blank squares are what they don't know about or have forgotten and need to be reminded of, in other words; windows of opportunity.

People who have carried out this exercise have almost without exception increased their turnover enormously – simply by educating their existing clients.

───────── PETER'S STORY ─────────

I've used the Magic Matrix with many of my clients when I'm consulting with them and, providing they take it seriously, it's never failed to work.

Eventually I twigged that the magic was to think about an area you take for granted and then use the matrix to generate information that would be of real value to the organisation.

Everyone understands Battleships. The grid couldn't be simpler. The real magic for me was realising this approach could be used for practically anything in life, not just business. Hence the reputation matrix.

Let's apply this same process to your reputation – and we can use the matrix in more than one way.

Matching your values to clients

Axis 1 (the left hand column) lists the values that underpin your organisation.

Axis 2 (the top row) shows your top 10 clients.

Put a cross in every square where you know that you have demonstrated that value to that client. All the blank squares are opportunities to build your values into your client relationships.

It's worth asking if they see you the same way you see yourself.

How you communicate with your clients

Axis 1 – lists all the different ways you can communicate with them (in person, phone, fax, e-mail, text, newsletters, direct mail, case studies, marketing flyers, PR, print media, YouTube, Facebook, Twitter, Linked In, Google+, My Space, Ecademy, Friend Feed, Stumbleupon, Digg, Reddit, Posterous, Plurk, Bebo, Friendster, Mashable, Delicious, Technorati, Mixx – and dozens of others.)

Axis 2 – lists your key clients.

Put a cross in the squares where you've used that method of communication with that client. All the blank squares are opportunities to communicate with them differently.

Do you know how they would like to be communicated with? Are there gaps you can close?

You can do this with a team:

Axis 1 – Various methods they use to communicate.

Axis 2 – Members of the sales team.

Who likes working with whom? Is the sales person's preferred method of communication acceptable to the recipient? What communication methods could be changed to improve relationships?

PETER'S STORY

The most important thing I've learned is learn to say same thing in a different way. It has, quite literally, changed my life and my business to adapt my methods of communication to the way my clients prefer.

It's one o'clock in the morning. Sara is very upset and has been crying. It's the night before her first GCSE exams and she's struggling – nothing is going in. She's bright, intelligent and has done her homework, but the pressure is getting to her, she just can't see the words on the paper.

Downstairs is Dad. He looks up and thinks, 'Sara's light is still on, doesn't she realise she has an exam in the morning? Better go see what the problem is.'

He goes upstairs. Sara is sitting on her bed, looking at her father for some comfort and advice.

What would you say?

'What's the problem?'

'How can I help you?'

Perhaps he gave her a hug?

He says, 'Don't be so bloody silly, don't you realise you have an exam in the morning, turn your light off and get to sleep!'

She gave him the look that only a woman can give a man – the look of 'you will wither and perish in hell!'

He looks at her and thinks, 'Uh oh.'

Did she turn the light off? No!

Did he get what he wanted? No!

Did she stay upset? Definitely.

What did he do?

Turned around and said, 'Bloody kids! They don't do anything I want them to do...' and went downstairs.

Did he go to sleep? No!

Next morning he thought, 'I blew that. It's her exams and it's important. How can I help her?'

There is a saying, 'When the pupil is ready the teacher will appear.'

Somebody lent him a tape made by a doctor who had four teenage daughters. There were some different ideas about how to get on with each other, based on personality. Good practical sound stuff, not mumbo jumbo. So, when she got home that evening, he'd listened to it, and thought, 'I'll try it. I'll try anything to help.'

So he said to her, 'Sara, you can be in charge, you can be in control, but when 11pm comes, I'd like you to turn out your light and go to sleep.'

She said, 'Yeah, OK.'

For the rest of the evening he was thinking, 'What a waste of time, this won't work.' Yet at 11pm she got up from her desk, walked up the stairs, shut her door and turned her light off, with her dad thinking, 'How did that happen?'

He thought, 'I'll try some more of this stuff!'

Dad started getting more involved, just to help, playing the tape in the car with the family listening, because they all wanted to help Sara get through a tough time.

One morning they're driving along listening to the tape. It was funny and entertaining too, which was even better. Then a voice piped up, 'Didn't you say that to me this morning?' It was Sara.

Silence and embarrassment in the car. 'Yes, well actually, love, I've been using this to help and er – look, I just wanted to help.'

Sara goes quiet for the longest five minutes of her life and says, 'This stuff is really good. You should learn more about it.'

So I did – because Sara is my elder daughter – if you hadn't already guessed.

That's what made me go to America to learn more about personality. I was taught one thing, a powerful phrase that's changed my personal life, my family life and my business life, and that is:

'You need to learn to say the same thing – but in a different way!'

It's an old phrase, you may have heard it before, but the point is, I hadn't heard it. I knew it, but I hadn't heard it. More, importantly, I wasn't using it.

When I said, 'Sara, you can be in charge, you can be in control, but when 11pm comes, I'd like you to turn out your light and go to sleep.' For the first time in my life, instead of looking through my eyes, I took my glasses off and looked at the world through my daughter's eyes. I spoke to her in language she was more comfortable with and it had an effect. It made a major difference.

When you create your axes, don't edit your lists. In 2005, Facebook and Twitter wouldn't have been on the list, but, like it or not, they are now; ignore them at your peril.

In today's world, contacting someone on your phone doesn't necessarily mean a phone call. In fact, it's well known that the iPhone is not the best telephone to make calls on, but it's not important when it does so many other things extremely well.

The steps to being in control of your brand

When you speak or write about your company – always do it with your target audience in mind; not so you can sell them something, but so that you understand them sufficiently well to know whether they might be interested in buying.

THE POINT OF THIS CHAPTER
Making a positive impact

Check out your opportunities and start filling in those gaps – you'll be surprised at how quickly your reputation will grow and your profit line will blossom along with it. However, you do need do this regularly or it will soon be forgotten. Make it part of your review and marketing processes.

As we've established the world is whirling faster when it comes to information; that hamster wheel is a lot bigger and a lot faster than it used to be. The means of communicating with people has multiplied and keeping up with it all can appear to be overwhelming.

You don't have to do your reputation management yourself though, you can get help. That's why there are so many social media consultants about and, of course, why Positive Ground and Inside News exist – to help people to cope.

Whether you get it wrong or get it right, it will make a dramatic difference to your company.

The reputation which the world
bestows is like the wind, that shifts
now her now there, its name changed
with the quarter whence it blows.

DANTE ALIGHIERI, FROM THE DIVINE COMEDY

Section 2

HOW TO MANAGE *YOUR* REPUTATION

CHAPTER 7

Reputation management – the basics

This chapter will take a look at some of the things that are really important for your reputation management – whatever type or size of business you're in.

The chapters that follow focus on the reputation management issues that affect different types of organisation – read the one that is closest to your situation – unless you're insatiably curious, in which case, read everything! You'll find that reading it all will give a better insight into how your clients and customers operate and will help you to help them.

There are a number of aspects that everyone in business needs to consider, such as:

- Personal appearance.
- Your business card.
- Business communications.
- Social media and online activity.
- How you (and your staff) interact with others.

Clothes maketh the man (or woman)

If you ripped your tie off or burned your shoulder pads when you left corporate life and thought 'Great, now I can wear what I feel comfortable in,' beware! If you work in a large organisation hidden in a back room somewhere and think nobody will notice what you wear, don't fall into the trap of forgetting that everything you do, including the way you dress, creates an image – not just with customers – but also with your colleagues.

Every one of us has a personal reputation regardless of how big the organisation in which we work.

Of course, it is particularly important to give some thought to how you dress when you appear as the representative of your business or organisation.

Some people seem to get away with murder and if you're in design or the web industries people almost expect you to turn up in jeans and a T-shirt, but if you're doing business with big organisations, they may not feel comfortable with someone wearing a different uniform to their own.

If you're offering business advice as a consultant, your clients will expect you to be fairly formal. That might be a suit (with or without a tie), but that image when you arrive for the meeting will make an impact. There's a case for parking the jacket over the back of your chair to create a more relaxed environment once you've established a working relationship, but the suit says 'professional' and 'business'.

If you work for a large organisation, you're carrying their reputation around with you everywhere you go – and, whether it's right or wrong, we all make judgments based on how people look.

You will have done it yourself, even if you don't want to admit it; when a crumpled, rumpled person is working for a company you're visiting, you'll instantly draw a conclusion about that person and, subconsciously, about the organisation and that individual's role in it.

Women have a tougher decision with a much more varied choice of clothes. A woman in a suit can appear intimidating to some people, but what are the alternatives?

- Dress and jacket?
- Trousers and some kind of top?
- Skirts – straight or full, long or short?
- Necklines – high, modest, revealing cleavage?
- Long sleeves, short sleeves, no sleeves?

There really isn't a simple uniform like the role the suit plays for men. In addition fashion for women tends to be much more extreme. One year shift dresses and platform shoes are acceptable, the next year floaty summer dresses and cardigans are in. It's hard to know what's

OK and what isn't. It can be worth the investment in having your colours done; it helps both women and men look better and provides pointers to the kind of outfits that fit and flatter. It saves those 'got to have it' purchases that stay in the wardrobe for years and end up at the charity shop.

LESLEY'S STORY

When I worked for Dubai Duty Free the boss was a real stickler for how everyone looked. All the staff, except the managers, wore a uniform. The uniform consisted of:

- *2 jackets*

- *4 pairs of trousers (men) or skirts (women)*

- *6 shirts or blouses,*

- *2 ties (men)*

- *a handbag (women)*

- *a belt*

- *2 pairs of shoes.*

The only things that weren't provided were underwear, socks or tights, however, the colour of socks and tights were specified and woe betide any member of staff who was discovered on the shop floor or in a public area without the full uniform. There were no rolled up sleeves, no jackets off and, if anyone dared appear in a black pair of trousers that weren't uniform, they were likely to be sent home to get changed and their pay docked for the time it took to do that!

I used to get little notes on my desk (I was HR Manager) asking why all the girls' legs were different colours! It didn't matter how much I explained that, with a multi-national staff their skins were all different colours and that affected the final effect, no matter what colour their tights were – he was adamant that everyone represented the organisation professionally.

He had been known to stop at a pick up point and tell staff waiting for the company bus to collect them to put their jackets on! This was in Dubai and, in the summer it could be 40°C with 100% humidity.

He didn't stop with the uniformed staff either. Male members of the management team were expected to wear long sleeved shirts and belts on their trousers. Female managers could not wear trousers and were

> expected to wear respectable necklines and nothing remotely see-through. He even stopped one very elegant female manager from wearing a beautiful designer black pleated skirt when he discovered that it was culottes.
>
> New managers quickly got the message and complied – and Dubai Duty Free had an international reputation for professionalism and success. We never had a problem finding good quality staff – everyone wanted to work for the organisation.

For most people it's best to err on the side of formal until you get a feel for your market. Peter Legge, a professional speaker from Canada, once did a presentation to the Professional Speaking Association members in London and said 'You should always be slightly better dressed than your audience'.

He wasn't advocating wearing an expensive suit if everyone else was in Bermuda shorts and casual shirts, but just looking as though you have an edge on them. The same applies in business.

It's as much about standards as anything else. Little things make a difference. Things like not wearing broken shoe laces[17], having a good watch (if you wear one), restrained jewellery, not big glittery, dangly stuff (unless of course you happen to be selling glittery, dangly jewellery) and that your overall grooming doesn't attract unnecessary attention. That means hairstyles, hand and nail care (yes, even for men) and polished shoes. Even the bag or briefcase you carry makes a statement about you. Have you ever watched a scatty businesswoman searching in the bottom of a huge bag for a pen and wondered how she manages to deliver a good service if she's obviously not very organised? We rest our case.

In fact, the pen you use to make notes also adds to your image and your reputation. If someone asks to borrow a pen, is the one you offer them 'give-backable'? If it's a cheap biro people forget to return it. If it's obviously a nice pen that has value, they usually return it promptly. It doesn't have to be a Mont Blanc fountain pen, just one that says you care about your accessories.

---

[17] The 10 Second Philosophy by Derek Mills has a lot of useful advice about this kind of thing.

In corporate life I was a regional sales manager and had a boss who was more interested in his image than our clients. He was a tidiness nut and was always running strips of sticky tape over his suit to remove any tiny bits of lint. His image was vastly important to him.

When I closed a huge major finance and leasing deal with a company in Scotland, the boss decided that he wanted to muscle in, along with the National Sales Director. They made a big issue out of the signing of the contract. The new customer's Finance Director was given a Mont Blanc pen to sign the contract. It was supposed to impress the new customer, but they hadn't tested the pen and it didn't work.

My boss was mortified that his grand gesture had fallen flat on his face, but fortunately the new customer thought it was amusing that he thought that was important. It actually forged a stronger relationship between us – and the boss lasted only a few months before he was handed his marching orders.

If you're a consultant you may find that you're in that kind of game.

There are exceptions that prove the rule – Brad Burton, MD of 4Networking[18] is well-known for wearing jeans and a T-shirt and admits to 'looking like a builder'. However, he relishes his not-suited image and it's become his trademark. He also enjoys people's reactions when they realise who he is, but it's not for everyone and wearing clothes that don't reflect your image can lose you more business than it gains.

Your business card

When you meet someone in business it's usual to exchange business cards and there are business cards of all shapes and sizes – getting it right can be a bit of a minefield.

Written material is Lesley's speciality so be prepared for a bit of a rant about what your business card says about you!

---

[18] http://www.bradburton.biz

I go to a lot of networking meetings and, at most of them, people either pass their business cards around the table or swap them during open networking sessions. At one particular group we used to meet every Friday morning and the lady who ran the group was a friend of mine, Glenys. She is from Salford and known for her frank and robust approach to networking and life in general!

After a few meetings she commented, 'I watch you when the cards come round and you don't even look at them at first. You just rub them with your fingers and, if they don't pass muster, your eyebrow goes up!'

I was a bit surprised as I've never been able to do that 'lift one eyebrow' trick, but I knew what she was talking about. I can tell a business card from one of those free card websites without even looking at it. It's usually really thin card.

Standard business cards come on a standard weight card, usually around 340gsm (grams per square metre). It's a good idea to use a slightly heavier card than your printer uses as standard: heavier cards subliminally say 'quality'. I use 400gsm card and it makes a real difference. Very thin cards say 'lightweight' and send a subconscious message about your business. It's always best to ask to see samples before choosing – or at least know what different weight cards feel like.

The other challenge to off-the-shelf cards – usually off-the-internet these days – is that there is a limited range of designs. In my early days of networking I had been to a few meetings and at one breakfast I sat next to a man who offered me his card. I looked at it and said 'I think I've met one of your colleagues'.

He looked surprised and responded 'I don't have any colleagues, I'm a sole trader. Why do you say that?'

'I was at another networking meeting recently and someone gave me a card exactly like this,' I explained. The card in question had a tree and a bit of landscape in the background. It turned out to be one of those freebie cards template designs.

Since then I've met many people who try to explain that they needed cards in a hurry and an internet service was quick and easy. In my mind it doesn't make a good excuse – it says that they don't plan ahead and cut corners.

How to get your business card right

If you give people a business card they start making judgments from the moment their fingers or eyes make contact with it.

We all pick up business cards without necessarily having time to find out much about the person that gave it to us. How do we remember a week later what Gill Bloggs of Express Services actually does?

If all your business card say is your company name and your name with a bit of fancy artwork you could be wasting your money on having cards printed – and in this time of cut budgets and cashflow getting tight, that's not good news.

So what *should* go on your card?

Your name should be clear and bigger than anything else (except the logo). It should be big enough for people to read easily – even without their reading glasses. If they didn't catch your name properly this allows them to take a quick look and make sure they've got it. We've all done this – not quite got someone's name – and it's embarrassing if you get it wrong or have to ask.

Put the name that you want to be called – for instance don't put Gillian Bloggs, if you prefer to be called Gill or Robert Fisher if everyone calls you Bob.

If you have letters after your name, think carefully whether they will help people to make a decision to call you again. If not, let the ego trip go. If you think that your qualifications help people to decide that you can deliver a better service (in some cultures they're very important) then by all means add them. Don't put a string of qualifications. Stick to one (or at the very most two) relevant designations.

It's not essential to have your title, but it could be helpful, especially in a larger organisation where there may be many people and departments and it helps to know which one your contact comes from. If you're a small business or a one-person organisation, it's probably not important to let people know you're the boss.

Your telephone number needs to be in a font that's big enough to read without a magnifying glass! If someone needs to contact you they should be able to do it easily. You don't want to miss out on a fantastic referral or introduction because they don't have a number to call. Give a landline and a mobile number.

A professional e-mail address and a web site address is essential. That means *not* a gmail, yahoo, aol, btinternet, hotmail or any other e-mail address of this type. If you want people to take you seriously, get your web designer to arrange for you to have an e-mail address that mirrors your web address.

A snail mail address (your actual mailing address) is advisable, but not essential. It doesn't matter if this is in a smaller font, but not so tiny that a microscope is needed.

If you have a fax number it doesn't really need to be on the card, unless, of course, you're in an industry that still uses this means of communication regularly for any reason. Very few people use fax these days and most have a facility that delivers faxes electronically as e-mails.

In today's world adding your key social media connections is more important.

Don't put so much information that it makes the card look cluttered. Less is more; it's better to have the key information in a bigger font than to cram lots of information in and use a tiny font.

You brand includes your logo and the choice of fonts you use. It should stand out, but not overpower. Your brand should be clean and sharp, even if you don't have a logo as such, your company name needs to be presented consistently, so the same font on everything (business card, letterhead, website, flyers, etc). The letters should also be the same colour, tone and shade on the same background colour too – if you are using a graphic designer he or she should be able to give you the pantone references for each of the colours that you use.

If you have a strapline that's even better. This helps people to understand what your company does. It's also useful to outline what kind of business you're in if your brand doesn't make that obvious, so people won't have to try and remember what 'Smith & Jones' actually do.

The back of your card is marketing space; don't waste it! If Gill Bloggs is a smart cookie she will have something on the back of her card that explains either what she does, or, better still, what the recipient of her services gets. In other words – the benefits.

What do I mean by benefits? It's the difference between 'We write copy for websites' and 'you'll get words that keep people on your website for longer'.

Make sure you use that marketing space on the back of your card, but leave some space around the edges for people to write where they met you and the date.

Keen networkers like to write information on the back of cards – that gets really difficult when the card is laminated or glossy; you're just making it difficult for them. When you write on a laminated or glossy finish the ink doesn't dry, it gets on your fingers and on your clothes. That doesn't win you any points with people who could be potential clients.

I bet you never thought getting a business card had so much to consider! It's always worth investing in a good business card – the moment you put it into someone else's hands it says volumes about you.

If you work for a large organisation and they haven't got this right then maybe let the marketing department borrow your copy of this book! Better still get them to buy their own copy.

Business communications

Business cards are important, they reinforce your actual image, but you need to make sure that *all* your stationery has a consistent brand. This includes:

- Your **letterhead** (even if it's an electronic document). The branding needs to look the same and, if you print it out or have it printed, it needs to be on good quality paper.

- Your **invoices** – they also need to be branded and have a uniform template with all the information your customer needs to know – your address, contact information, due date and, of course, how to pay you.
- **Marketing material** – flyers, brochures, postcards, etc. They all need to present a consistent brand and quality look and feel.
- Your **website** – again, the brand should match everything else and it should look professional. Your website is where people go to check you out – it's worth investing a little in a professional design and some well-written content that is focused on your potential client.
- Your **e-mail signature** – everyone should have a consistent structure and layout so that if people are dealing with more than one department there's a 'joined-up' image.

This is something that's important for companies of all sizes – whether you're an independent consultant or a big corporate. There's an assumption that large organisations have got all this stuff taped, but it isn't always as simple as that. Even worldwide multi-nationals, who do have manuals on how a letter should be laid out and the company approach to how to address people and sign off e-mails, don't always check that their staff are following these guidelines.

If the communications that your customer receives are inconsistent a seed may be planted about how joined up your services will be. If you can't get something as simple as a letter laid out properly it doesn't bode well for bigger projects!

Social media and online activities

It's good practice for every organisation to have a social media policy. This applies whether you're a sole trader or a conglomerate, however, the policy will be very different depending on what size your business is and how many staff you employ. There's more about this in the following chapters with relevant advice for each type of business.

However, on a personal level every person who works in any kind of business needs to have an awareness of their online image.

Beware of what you post

Whether you are a new business or working in an international organisation, it's a good move to take a good look at your personal social media. People can find you in many different places and, if you've been accepting Facebook friends, Linked In contacts and getting Twitter followers without stopping to consider whether you actually know people or not – some of your potential clients may have access to every bit of your social activities.

Both of us have had experience of the negative effects of social media one way or another – as well as the hugely positive outcomes it can create.

Lesley: *A business connection commented on a picture that one of my contacts had posted on my wall 'Your friend should put some clothes on.'*

Peter: *I noticed a business connection's Facebook account and what he had been doing over the weekend certainly wasn't anything like what he did in business. The key word here is CONGRUENCY – or, in this case, a complete lack of it!*

You are dependent on your personal good name to keep your reputation clean. This means that you either need to make sure that nobody in your network is in your business pool (a really difficult and time-consuming activity) or that everything you post is something you'd be happy to have people read.

Few people check out their privacy settings on social media platforms and are often astonished to discover that everything in their profile is open to public view. People are often oblivious to the fact that the default settings on Facebook leave them wide open. Peter's daughter, Sara-Beth (Business Manager for Positive Ground), is particularly hot on this subject with all her clients.

The danger is not necessarily what you post, but what all your 'friends' post – that appears on your wall. If you manage your settings you can prevent your connections posting pictures that you would prefer not to be tagged in. You can also ensure that your wall is seen only by people that you want to see it.

Managing your reputation online means never making negative comments about other individuals, thinking carefully before posting trivia about your day-to-day life, avoiding the computer (and the smart phone) when you've been out celebrating and had a few drinks.

This doesn't mean you can't share some of your personal activities, but be careful and always think 'would I want my customers (or boss) to know this?' before you hit 'submit'.

As a business owner you want your reputation to be unsullied. As an employee you want any research your employers (or potential employers) do into your background to come up clean as a whistle. As we've said earlier – once it's published, Google or one of the other search engines will find it. It's part of your digital footprint and it's forever!

Handsome is as handsome does

This is a phrase our grandmothers used to use – in essence it means that your actions tell people whether you are all you appear to be!

Whilst we do adjust our behaviour to the people that we are currently talking with, we don't usually become someone completely different. The secret of a successful business is *consistent behaviour*. People need to know where they stand with you and every experience they have of you adds to their picture of who you are.

This means that if you're willing to give people information, help to connect them with other people who can help them or make suggestions about possible opportunities for them, it all adds to your reputation.

If you are in the situation where you can't help someone because you can't meet their deadline, budget or don't have specific resources, never be afraid to recommend someone else that you trust. It will add to your reputation and feature in that person's future conversations when discussing possible suppliers of the products or service you offer.

LESLEY'S STORY

I've been taking my car to a local garage for years, it's run by Chris and Colin – not surprisingly, known as C&C Motors. They've always done a good job, charged much less than I often expected and have been friendly and easy to deal with. Of course, I've recommended lots of people to them (and I'm sure their other customers have too as they are always busy and it can be hard to get through on the phone sometimes).

A friend has this huge American El Camino and needed an MOT. I asked Chris if he could do it – or if he wanted to, as I know American cars are a bit different to the usual varieties we get over here.

He said 'It's not that we don't want to, but our MOT inspection lift isn't long enough to get it on.'

Instead of leaving me to then try to find a garage willing and able to do the job, he immediately suggested a competitor not far away. 'They've got a bigger lift and he'll have no problem doing that,' he assured me.

Now I'm not only raving about C&C as a garage, but also about their generosity of spirit!

When you're networking be willing to help other people by connecting them, recommending them and giving them advice, feedback and suggestions. However, always check that people are open to the latter before giving them the benefit of your opinion!

Lesley's English teacher made the whole class write on their English exercise book 'Do unto others as you would have them do unto you'. An even better phrase is 'do unto others as they would like to be done unto'!

In other words find out how people like to be treated and deliver just what they want. It will win you a lot of gold stars on the reputation monitor!

THE POINT OF THIS CHAPTER
This is just for starters

This chapter has been a general guide to get you started with the basics of good reputation management. The next four chapters will look at reputation management for:

- Independent consultants and sole traders
- SMEs
- Corporate organisations
- Social enterprises.

These dig into some of the issues that are specific to each type of organisation. Read the one that applies to you – or read them all if you want to pick up some tips from other types of business!

Ones reputation is like a shadow,
it is gigantic when it precedes you,
and a pigmy in proportion when it follows.

CHARLES MAURICE DE TALLEYRAND

CHAPTER 8

Reputation Management for the independent consultant or sole trader

When you're a sole trader or an independent consultant your brand is absolutely YOU and there's nowhere to hide.

If it's your first foray into business it's so easy to make errors of judgment – or simply get things wrong because you hadn't thought about them.

Whether you like it or not, everything you do is about your image to your potential clients, advocates and suppliers. Failing to think about the detail can have a big effect on the success of your new enterprise.

Talk to a few people at networking events and you'll see everything from the people who started a business by accident and have a topsy-turvey collection of bits of branding to those who have a slick, successful and joined-up image.

There are people who turned over two million in their first year and people who are still struggling to make ends meet in Year Six, not to mention the ones that failed and are part of the statistics of businesses that didn't make it to year three.

PETER'S STORY

When I started out in business I got a client really quickly and hadn't even decided what the business name should be. I needed a name to invoice them. I'd just been to CenterParcs and came up with a real brainwave – my initials – PAR – Consultancy Solutions – PARCS!

I could have done much better with a little hindsight, but PARCS we were and, eventually, became PARCS Ltd. I was stuck with it!

Coming out of the corporate world, I was green as grass and did what I

> *was told. My accountant said, 'Buy a Merc; it's tax deductible'. I didn't really like Mercedes, but I did as I was told and had people saying, 'Gosh, you're doing well!'*
>
> *There was a big discussion amongst my friends about whether or not I should be a limited company, whether I should be VAT registered and, of course, many conflicting views as to what was best. Like I said, it's easy to get it wrong – or to get it right by chance.*
>
> *I thought my accountant would take care of me – until I received a five figure tax bill a week before it was due to be paid. Going Limited cost me a fortune and, after some time, we decided to go Unlimited and become a partnership. Our accountant said it was a good idea and failed to point out that the benefits of offsetting significant losses against the business would be lost in this process. In the end we paid twice as much as we needed to – thousands. Needless to say we changed accountants too[19].*

We've all heard people waxing lyrical about the joys of self-employment. The benefits of being able to work whilst still wearing pyjamas often ranks up there as a real benefit – but do you know what you *sound* like when you're wearing pyjamas?

If you think we've lost it completely at this point, consider this: when you're wearing your best outfit, all ready for a formal night out, do you notice that the way you speak alters slightly? Most of us speak a little more formally when we're all dressed up. It's not acting a part (well, maybe it is – a bit), it's just that our clothes reflect the situation we're in and we respond accordingly.

It you're in business clothes – whatever they are for you – then you'll find you'll speak differently to how you do when you're relaxing with your family or friends. It's not conscious – it's just how we are. So, how do you sound when you answer the phone wearing pyjamas?

Come to that, how do you answer the phone anyway? If you're starting out working from home there's a good possibility that you're using your home phone as your business contact number. Do you answer it with:

- 'Hello'?
- 'Good morning (or afternoon)?'

---

[19] The story behind this is in Running on Empty.

- Your name?
- 'How may I help you?'

Or something else? What happens when someone else in your family picks up a call? Does it sound professional?

Peter's children were all taught to answer the phone with the number, their name and 'how can I help you?' almost from the cradle. This made a great impression when Dad worked from home and, not surprisingly, has carried through to the family business today.

Lesley almost filed for divorce when her husband, who also worked from home, used to answer the phone they shared with 'Hello?' or, worse still, 'Battersea Dogs Home'!

We'd recommend you have a separate telephone line for your business – it's worth the small extra cost – and answer it in the same way you would if you were a large organisation. Generally, this is usually:

'Good morning, Acme Widgets, how may I help you?'

If you prefer you can replace the company name with your name – in the same way you would if you were answering a direct dial number in a larger company.

'Hello, Grant Goodyer; how may I help you?'

If you're beginning to think that there's a lot of detail – we haven't even got started yet.

Everything in Chapter 7 applies to you, even if you're working from your kitchen table – reputation is about how you appear to the outside world, particularly your potential clients, other business people who may recommend or refer you and suppliers with whom you want to work.

There is absolutely nothing wrong with working from home – and in today's digital world, many corporate employees work, at least part of the time, from home. It's all in how you present yourself and your business.

Your business image

When people meet you on neutral ground – at a networking meeting, somewhere you've arranged to meet for coffee or lunch, or at a conference or exhibition – they'll make a visual assessment.

Whilst we're on the subject of venues – take care where you meet. Quite apart from choosing somewhere that reflects your image (so a decent coffee shop rather than a transport caff), think about the issues of being overheard too.

The next thing that will influence people's opinion of you is any material you put in their hands. We've already banged on about business cards – read Chapter 7 carefully and don't fall into the trap of thinking that a mass-produced business card on a standard template from the internet will do for now.

Every time someone says to me 'I had to get some cards done quickly so I just got these to tide me over'; there's a subtext going on that says 'I didn't do much planning ahead and threw things together'. Is this how they manage their business? More important, is this the way they'll work with me as a potential client?

However, there are many other pieces of marketing material that also influence the person into whose hands they are placed.

Flyers
They need to be properly designed and printed on decent paper so that they deliver your message professionally. There's nothing worse than something that's obviously been printed off on your office laserjet on 80gsm copy paper.

Postcards
Don't try and print them on index cards – it just makes them look amateurish. The quality of card available from stationery shops is dramatically different to what a proper printer has available. With digital print you no longer need to have hundreds printed if you only need a few – shop around your local print services.

Brochures
If you want a simple trifold (A4 sheet folded into three) don't fall into

the trap of trying to squeeze in everything about your services or products. Remember who it's for and write for the audience with whom you want to connect. A trifold will need:

- An 'open me' headline on the front;
- A few bullet pointed benefits on the first fold in;
- Your key audience-engaging message in the centre section inside:
- Supporting information on the left section;
- Some company background or further usual information on the right hand section;
- Contact information and a call to action on the back.

Printed on a good weight paper or card, a brochure can look very professional. If it's poorly laid out, jammed with too much information and printed on flimsy copy paper it just looks cheap.

If you have a range of products or services, you may want to have a book style brochure. Remember that the layout for hard copy and the layout for digital presentation are very different and you really need an expert to ensure you get your message in the right place on each.

It's better not to have a brochure at all and create bespoke proposals or quotations than to have a cheap and cheerful brochure that will establish your reputation firmly at the bottom end of the market.

If all this sounds like marketing advice – what do you think reputation management is about?

Social media – and online activities

If you've read the preceding chapter you should have a really good idea of how to protect yourself online. However, if you suffer from the 'fingers faster than brain' syndrome (if you're one of those people who hit send *before* you've added the attachment, you'll know what we mean) it's worth investing some time in thinking how you will approach your online activities.

This isn't just about being careful about what you say. It's about planning how to create the reputation you want.

Whilst, without staff, it's probably not necessary to have a formal social media policy just for you. It is important to have thought about:

- What you want to achieve with your social media and online activities.
- Where your target audience hang out.
- How you can engage with them without alienating them.
- How you can raise awareness of who you are and what you deliver.
- How you want people to perceive you.
- How much time you are prepared to invest in all this.

Knowing what to post is at least as important and you should be considering including:

- Sharing your knowledge in the form of tips and advice
- Recommending other people you rate
- Sharing information you've found useful – blogs, articles, websites, YouTube videos
- Answering other people's questions

This will develop your reputation as an expert and fount of information – which is always a good way for people to see you!

Some people dabble and then give up and miss an opportunity. Here are some reasons why developing your reputation online is important:

- People who may have met you once – years ago – will remember you if they see you posting regularly. When they want what you offer they will come to you, not someone else who isn't as visible (or the dreaded yellow pages or yell.com). Lesley has had several clients who have come to her via Twitter – because they've been reminded of what she is good at – and have then shared their satisfaction with an online testimonial too!

- People who see you sharing your knowledge online will see you as someone who knows their stuff and with that as validation are much more likely to recommend you. You can't possibly see every post or status update that asks for a particular type of help, but people to whom you're connected sometimes spot one – and suggest that the person contacts you.

- Demonstrating your knowledge online can result in speaking, training or other offers to spread your words of wisdom even further. We know people who have been asked to present at local events, write books on their specialist subject and have had offers of sponsorship from companies who want to be associated with their kind of expertise.

- Don't expect to make direct sales – but it's not unheard of, and subtle marketing can make sales if handled carefully.

FOR EXAMPLE:

Alan Stevens is a well-known media coach (www.mediacoach.co.uk) and a keen advocate of social media (he's even written a book about it called Ping). He has a habit of running Twitter media clinics. If he's in a coffee shop between meetings he tweets: 'Ask me your media questions and I'll answer'. He has a healthy following on Twitter and is a respected professional speaker.

Alan was doing a presentation in Derby and staying in a hotel. Returning from his gig he found a pair of elephants on his bed, made from towels. He hadn't seen anything like this before and took a picture of them with his mobile phone. He posted the picture on Twitter and several people responded, including a presenter from BBC Radio Derby who tweeted, 'I feel a feature on towel origami coming on!'

Alan commented on her tweet and as a result she invited him to come in and be interviewed – on his specialist subject (not towel origami).

He accepted her invitation and – as a media professional – delivered a fantastic interview.

Soon after this he had two bookings for paid speaking engagements as a result of the radio interview.

Alan's take on Twitter is that it's not a sales platform – but a means of making connections which can then be followed up offline. As this story demonstrates – it works.

Everything you post contributes to your online profile – and to your Google ranking. Try googling your name and see how many of your social media profiles and posts appear at the top end of the list.

All this will have a direct impact on your online reputation and, if you get it right, your business profitability too.

THE POINT OF THIS CHAPTER
Putting it all together

It doesn't matter how small your business is, your reputation will be affected by everything you do, how you look and what you use to promote yourself.

It's not a luxury to have good stationery and professional marketing material – it just makes you look good.

Regardless of whether you think that going into business for yourself allows you to do your own thing, you do need to take account of what your target audience expects and how much doing your own thing might affect them – you don't want to alienate people who might pay for your services!

Constant awareness of what you say both in person and on various public platforms is wise as it all affects your reputation and people's perception of what kind of person you are. When you are your brand, that means your business reputation too.

Actions really do speak louder than words – make sure yours say the right thing.

Him, therefore, they retained, on account
of his lively genius and good reputation,
and dismissed the others.

GERVASE OF CANTERBURY
ON THE APPOINTMENT OF WILLIAM OF SENS AS ARCHITECT
OF THE NEW WORK AT CANTERBURY CATHEDRAL IN 1174.

CASE STUDY – KEVIN GASKELL

Kevin has had many years of experience in the corporate environment as a senior executive and already has an awareness of the power of reputation management. However, life is different as an independent consultant.

'Now I don't have a corporate PR machine running around me, giving me guidance on what I should – and shouldn't – say in public. Big company PR offers some good lessons, but doesn't work in quite the same way for an individual,' he observes.

When Kevin launched his independent consultancy he spent a lot of time considering how to present himself. This included how the website would look, the messages that informed potential clients, the topics he would speak on and even the companies he was willing to work with. He comments 'I spent a disproportionate length of time worrying about headed paper, business cards (heavy card but with interesting photo or not?) and other details which I believe establish credibility if presented properly.

'I worked very hard on the content of my speeches – my first speech took almost a month to write – as I firmly believe the maxim which states that you only have one opportunity to make a positive first impression. I wanted to protect and develop the positive reputation that I felt I had built in 25 years as a corporate executive.'

Having taken the time to think things through he still considers it time well spent and would advise any new business to stop and think before taking that first public step.

'Make sure you understand what it is that you are trying to sell to the world. What is the value that your product or service provides and what are the values or principles that you wish to be seen to be displaying? Only once you have fully defined your complete marketing strategy, including that of yourself, can you begin the key action of communicating it to the prospective audience.

'Your reputation will be formed by the consistent alignment of your presentation and behaviour with your chosen product and brand values. This consistency and coherence will help to build your credibility and your audience's confidence in your overall product or service.'

He admits that he does a lot to manage his reputation, choosing carefully the contracts he will and won't get involved in. He will only work with businesses that he feels are a good 'fit' as his clients' reputation impacts on him directly.

'I pause before I say 'yes' to anything,' he explains.

Kevin not only has his own reputation to consider, but that of his clients. As a chairman and board member of a handful of companies, he has to switch gears from his personal reputation to that of the organisation he represents.

He is a frequent networker offline and is very aware of the importance of delivering a consistent message. He is conscious of the impression he makes on the people he meets at networking events and actively seeks out opportunities to meet interesting people to extend his knowledge and stay up-to-date with the markets in which he operates.

'At a basic level I do aim to maintain appropriate dress sense and at all times try to be open and approachable. As the saying goes, I was gifted with one mouth and two ears and I believe I should use them in those ratios. It is amazing what people will tell you – if you are prepared to listen!'

As far as online media is concerned Kevin admits that he was banned from Facebook for years – by his children! Initially he had mixed feelings about social media – whilst it's an important communication medium, it can also be a big time-wasting device. However, he has developed an appreciation of how social media can enhance a business's profile and uses a professional consultant to help him to create the strategy and application that will make it work effectively for him.

'It's easier for an individual to manage; my clients are bigger organisations and have to have very clear policies so that everyone understands how to represent the company positively and effectively,' he says.

Kevin's consultancy offers support, guidance and education for leadership teams so he is very conscious of the impact of a few unthinking words. His own credibility as an ethical, knowledgeable and proactive individual has to be reflected in everything he says and does. 'As an independent consultant the buck really does stop here, there's nobody else to take the blame if I speak before I consider the impact of what I'm saying.'

More about Kevin Gaskell is on his website: http://www.kevingaskell.com.

CHAPTER 9

Reputation management for the SME

Big oaks from little acorns grow. Big corporations started life as a SME at some point. This means that you need to start as you mean to go on; it's really tough to change the way people do things once they've got into a habit.

This means that – even before you start recruiting your first member of staff – you need to have established what you expect from them in relation to the company's reputation.

In fact, back up a step. When you are recruiting new staff, don't forget to check out their online activity. It will be a good indicator as to how they manage their personal reputation and ensure you dot the Is and cross the Ts if you have any reservations before they start work for you.

We recommend that you read Chapter Eight as a good place to start, but the minute you start employing people you need to have a simple social media policy in place. The big companies usually have a comprehensive social media policy, but the kind of policy that they have isn't appropriate for a small organisation.

We all know people who work for bigger organisations and abuse their employer by spending far more than their break time updating Facebook and Twitter for personal reasons. Some bigger organisations ban social media use, but that's not good business for two reasons:

- If you treat people like children they will respond accordingly and simply use their smartphones to access their social media – and, possibly, brag about putting one over on their employer.
- If you stop people using social media at work, you're missing an opportunity for them to use it positively to promote your business.

The challenge for all businesses, but particularly smaller ones, is to get it right from day one and then keep the momentum going.

Our advice is to treat people like adults – lay out the 'rules' (your social media policy) and explain how you would like them to use the world of the web and then trust them to stick to that.

That doesn't mean abdicating any responsibility. It's part of your job to monitor your reputation so a weekly search of the web for comments about your organisation, you personally and, possibly, individuals on your team is good practice.

If you discover members of staff who don't comply with the social media policy they've agreed to, then you – and they – must know exactly what action you will take if they step over the acceptable line. This may differ depending on the type of transgression.

A social media policy for small businesses

So what do you need to consider when creating a simple social media policy?

How you will train and educate staff
This can include written dos and don'ts, a briefing session, sitting down in front of the computer with them and demonstrating how you do things and showing them what you expect from them.

How much you allow and expect staff to use it, and for what
This might be specifying that staff should only use social media for personal reasons during their lunch break. Some larger organisations actually prevent access during normal working hours, but open the tubes between 12 noon and 2.30pm.

However, if you educate staff properly you don't need to dictate that way. If you encourage them to post positive information about the organisation then they could actually have a beneficial effect.

There is an argument that individuals tend to have largely social networks, but people forget that everyone knows people socially who have jobs or businesses. The number of times you hear stories about a business owner who has been trying to get into a particular organisation to present their services, only to discover, often months later, that their brother-in-law's father is a senior manager there, proves this beyond doubt.

People just don't explore their social networks for business connections, and yet these are the very people who will usually give you a very warm introduction. When you have staff, those networks can be invaluable – but you need to teach people to use them.

How do you monitor usage?

The last thing you want is to be peering over people's shoulders all day – it makes them uncomfortable and won't encourage them to be proactive with their work generally if they think you're always on their case.

However, you do need to keep half an eye on what they're saying from time to time.

It's an extended version of the clause that used to be common in company policies about what is said about the company externally. Maligning the company whilst out of the office was considered to be gross misconduct and a disciplinary offence in many organisations.

Part of your social media policy needs to cover what the penalties are for:

- Using social media for personal use during working hours.
- Posting negative comments about the organisation anywhere.
- Sharing confidential information on the web (or in any other way).

On the other hand don't forget to thank people when they post good stuff that helps the organisation or make business connections on your behalf. Recognising them will encourage them to do more of the same.

When things don't work

There was a time when what you said about the company whilst you were down the pub with friends was unlikely to get back to the boss.

In today's world people are posting Tweets and status updates on Facebook on their smartphones from the pub with zillions of people listening. Worse still – if you've been having a few drinks, as good sense is often the first casualty.

LESLEY'S STORY

When I worked for Ecademy, it was an unusual social network in that it was moderated and there was a visible complaints system. There were a few professional complainers and some individuals who were always embarking on minor skirmishes, but also many people who were passionate about Ecademy and would flag up inappropriate posts – even in the middle of the night.

On one occasion, someone posted something completely unacceptable on a forum at 1 am. The next morning I found a few complaints in the Best Practice inbox. As I knew the person concerned, I decided it was easier to have a friendly chat, rather than e-mail him a reprimand.

It went something like this:

'Hi, this is Lesley. What are you trying to do to me, posting daft comments on the forum?'

'Oh, Hi Lesley – which post do you mean?'

I read him the comment.

'Really, did I post that? I remember thinking it, but I don't remember posting it.'

'How many whiskies were you on?' I asked (in a friendly tone).

'No whisky,' he replied, 'but I might have had a glass or two of wine.'

He took the post down and everyone was happy – but on many forums it's not possible to remove what you've posted.

Even people who have press agents and should know better, like celebrities, forget who is listening. Comedian Jimmy Carr's 2012 tax affairs fiasco and X-Factor judge, Tulisa, mouthing off have both hit the international media as a result of their posts on Twitter.

However, today you don't have to be a celebrity to get your indiscretions broadcast to the world. If a member of your staff says something stupid it travels far and fast. A reporter is anybody with a smart phone.

Your reputation is no longer limited to everyone in the local community who knows you – in 140 characters, people on every continent know you – and talk about you to the people they know.

A small business can't afford to take the hit by getting it wrong. It can destroy your reputation bring your business to its knees so be clear about what is and isn't acceptable.

THE POINT OF THIS CHAPTER
Getting it right

We're not trying to scare you off using social media and encouraging your staff to do so. Lots of new start ups are using new techniques and social media is an integral part of this. Thinking about what you want to achieve and how you'd like your employees to use the web is essential to give you the best chance of getting it right.

Some business owners are worried about what could go wrong, but as all good personal development coaches will tell you, you get what you expect, so expect the best.

If you don't trust the people you employ, why would you want them working for you?

It's up to you to create the kind of culture you want. As we said at the beginning of this chapter, a small business could be the Corporate of tomorrow; if you get this part of your reputation management right you'll be an organisation that people want to work for.

The purest treasure mortal times
afford Is spotless reputation

WILLIAM SHAKESPEARE RICHARD II ACT 1 SCENE1

CASE STUDY – ESTUARY LOGISTICS

When Estuary Logistics was launched in 2010, James Circus had strong feelings about the kind of service he wanted to offer. Image was important from day one.

He invested in professional branding with a smart identity and good quality stationery. He also joined the British International Freight Association, which is unusual in a new shipping organisation, to give him credibility and help to give new clients peace of mind.

James's approach to business is reflected in every member of his team.

'I employ like-minded people, who understand what I'm aiming for and embrace that way of doing business,' he says. 'The highest level of customer service is not something you can stick on; people have to think that way. I only employ people who are excited about giving that service.'

His team of hand-picked shipping experts demonstrate this in everything they say and do – as does the support team.

At present there are no written policies relating to reputation management, but James is aware that there will come a time when the organisation grows too big to rely on recruiting people with the right attitude alone.

This emphasis on the approach to customers has extended to their chosen business partners. They've entered into a service partnership with Go-Logistics, based in New Zealand and Australia. Both companies have a similar attitude to giving the customer a first class service. The phrase 'whatever it takes' underpins both organisations.

Estuary offers a 24/7 service, which, even in a business that operates in just about every time zone, is unusual. They have a system that means there is always someone knowledgeable available to help customers who have queries, emergencies or concerns.

Whilst James doesn't do a lot of business networking, 99% of his business comes from referrals and recommendations from existing clients, which says a lot about how much his customers appreciate the level of service. The new sales team is aiming to change the ratios – but to add to the business rather than reduce the recommendations!

'All our customers have worked with other freight companies. They like the service they get with us, because they know we will always go the extra mile, so they recommend us,' explains James.

In the freight business competition is fierce and confidentiality is a big issue. Protecting customers' identities is important; James and his team will never discuss one customer with another. In fact, they don't even reveal who their customers are without the customer's permission – trust is a big issue.

Estuary are taking their first steps into social media as they have identified that one of their target customer bases uses it a lot and have started exploring Facebook and Twitter. However, they are taking it slowly, as they are very aware of the danger of unguarded posts.

When it comes to overcoming challenges, Estuary hasn't had any major problems to combat.

'In the freight business there are challenges when shipments get delayed, so of course there's been the occasional problem, but our approach is that we sort things out so the client doesn't suffer and we've always been able to deal with glitches.'

The company's practice is to get feedback from their customers, and a recent small organisation felt that whilst the service was very professional, they would have liked a more friendly, chatty approach. The team have taken this on board and finding out exactly how the client likes to be treated has now become part of their service ethic.

James has invested in a business coach/mentor virtually from the start and has found that invaluable, especially as the company has grown so fast. This helps him remain objective and manage the business, rather than being caught up in the day-to-day operation. He is therefore always aware of how the organisation is perceived and is able to concentrate on developing its reputation.

More about Estuary Logistics is on their website: http://www.estuarylogistics.com

CHAPTER 10

Reputation management for the corporate organisation

Reputation is established by many different types of media. Every advertisement, article, marketing flyer and press release contributes to an organisation's reputation. Every letter or e-mail that goes out affects the recipient's perception – and there really isn't any excuse for not checking the spelling, grammar and punctuation.

However, today there is one element that has a huge impact on every organisation's reputation – social media. All the old marketing material on hard copy still works, but social media works faster and reaches further. An enlightened organisation will harness the power of social media to improve their reputation.

The bigger the organisation, the harder it is to keep track of every employee's social media activity. The key to successful management of social media activity is to lay out the ground rules from the start. This means a social media policy that is thoroughly understood by every member of staff.

There are some social media policies that go on – and on – and on – and on. As we all know, people don't read long policies and certainly don't remember the detail, so our advice is to create simple and straightforward statements that, at the very least, give people a checklist to ensure they stay on track.

Where certain activities are unacceptable to the organisation, it's wise to also specify what the penalties will be if someone carries out any of these activities.

What should be included in a good social media policy?

This would be our checklist – the overview – with underpinning information available for those who want to check the detail.

- The organisation's expectations on how social media will benefit the business.
- Be a good citizen of the online community – be courteous, helpful and calm.
- Add value – share your knowledge and expertise.
- Be real – use your real name and identify yourself with the organisation.
- Always think before posting – you're entitled to your opinion, but consider how you present it. Take responsibility for what you write and consider your reputation as well as that of the organisation. Good judgment is essential.
- Think about your audience – clients, suppliers, former clients, future clients, potential employees and people who will recommend the organisation to others – ensure posts will not alienate any of these people.
- Don't plagiarise others' work – always attribute accurately and observe any copyrights.
- Protect confidential information.
- Don't neglect the responsibilities attached to your role, they must take priority over social media activity.

What social media can do for a business

As company policies tend to be full of what you *can't* do, the tendency may be to list all the things to be avoided rather than what should be encouraged.

To get real buy-in and engagement from your staff, it's important to focus instead on how they will benefit and what they *can* do, instead of putting together a list of what they must *not* do.

Social media is about collaboration, support, helping each other and sharing; a social media policy needs to reflect that.

Outline how your organisation wants to be represented and what information can be shared.

Some organisations actively use social media to improve their customer relationships and, if this is part of your plan, you will need to outline who will be responsible for dealing with this, how it will be monitored and what response should be made.

This is an example of how smart organisations enhance their reputations using social media to improve customer service:

A middle-aged couple, let's call them Bob and Betty, returned from a shopping trip and Betty realised she had left her glasses behind. After a few moments thought, she worked out that it had been in Argos whilst she had been looking at the catalogues.

She had picked up the Twitter habit from her daughter and sat down with a cuppa and tweeted:

> *Just got home to find I've left my glasses in Argos – now I'll have to go all the way back to get them.*

Within minutes she received a tweet from @ArgosHelpers:

> *Which branch did you leave them in? Let us know and we'll make sure they're kept safe for you to collect.*

Many larger organisations monitor mentions of their name to ensure they respond to customer issues quickly.

LESLEY'S STORY

I use Hootsuite to manage my social media and one day I saw someone who had retweeted a singing blog – the Ballad of Barclaycard[20]. I clicked the link and there was a video clip of the blog owner singing about his friend's (very negative) experience with Barclaycard.

The lyrics were written out under the video clip – just in case you didn't get the message loud and clear.

This is the conversation that followed:

---

[20] http://stopdoingdumbthingstocustomers.com/poor-customer-service/ballad-of-barclaycard

Doug Shaw July 15, 2010 at 7:02 am

At approximately 7pm on July 14th Barclaycard started following me on Twitter. What next?

Sara July 16, 2010 at 3:20 pm

Hi Doug,

It's Sara here from the Barclaycard PR team. Firstly, we think you've got a real talent for songwriting! Secondly, your friend is obviously having difficulties with Barclaycard so we want to help. We followed you on Twitter and asked that you follow back so we can send you a direct message. However if you would prefer us to leave this alone then we will respect that. Just wanted your friend to know that we're here to help if they need us.

If we can help please follow us back on Twitter and we can DM you,

Thanks

Sara

Doug Shaw July 16, 2010 at 4:31 pm

Hi Sara – thank you soooo much for getting in touch. I will follow you on Twitter and I'm sure we can connect the right people – sort this out and then sing a nice reprise together!

Cheers for now – and thanks again for the contact

Doug

Doug Shaw July 16, 2010 at 4:33 pm

Just done it – now following Barclaycardnews

Sara July 16, 2010 at 5:08 pm

Hi Doug, I've just sent you a DM with some contact details, if you can send over a bit more information that would be great.

Thanks,

Sara

Ps, not sure my singing voice is up to a reprise but I play a mean tambourine

> *Doug Shaw July 19, 2010 at 9:04 am*
>
> *Hi Sara – I've passed on your details and encouraged my friend to get in touch. On the subject of encouragement, I'm encouraged too by the way this is evolving. Several people have commented to me via other channels over the weekend about the Barclaycard response so far, like me they are encouraged, and broadly positive. Thanks again for your time so far.*
>
> *Doug*
>
>
> *Doug Shaw July 21, 2010 at 8:34 am*
>
> *Good news! My friend has been in touch with Barclaycard and they've helped to solve the problem. The note below explains...*
>
> *'Hi Doug – Angela from the director's office called me today and within two hours had resolved my debit mandate issue. Turns out that the person who was tasked to set it up didn't know how and therefore it was never done correctly. They have now identified this and training will be given.*
>
> *They have also gone on to three credit agency websites to update my credit rating which was obviously bad seeing the rest of the world didn't think I was paying off my credit card since Feb!*
>
> *My thanks to you – if it hadn't been for the dramatic and creative way you got their attention, I would still be sitting here with a diminishing life expectancy as a result of the stress and hitting my head against a brick wall.*
>
> *What is the solution for the man in the street?????*
>
> *Cheers and the next round is on me!'*

Not only did the issue get sorted, but the Barclaycard people demonstrated a real interest in getting things sorted out, sensitivity in the way in which help was offered and a sense of humour too. This was a great demonstration of social media enabling customer service to go beyond most people's expectations.

Many large corporates monitor social media to allow them to pick up issues before they become viral.

Being a good citizen of the online community

The online community stretches all around the world and allows people who, a decade ago, would never have known of each other's existence, to develop a friendship. Every individual creates a personality by what they write in their posts on social media.

Being a good citizen is about being willing to help others, responding to questions where you can provide useful information, connections or advice, sharing knowledge and information to help other people where you can.

This means giving as well as taking. The more you share, the more people are likely to respond if you ask for help.

Promoting an ethos of reasoned response will also help people not to get drawn into emotional exchanges or posting something that they will regret later. Courtesy and respect should be kept in mind – regardless of what other people are posting.

Encouraging the people in your organisation to operate in this way on social networks will help both the organisation and the individual personally to develop a positive profile.

Over time it also develops a band of dedicated followers who are happy to recommend both the organisation and the people within it.

The aim is for customers and others to feel comfortable connecting with your organisation and staff to get help and information when they need it.

Adding value

This is the art of knowledge information education and, if you get it right, it can be a very effective way of winning lots of new friends and followers.

Adding value is easily done by sharing existing knowledge either in the form of tips or useful links where people can find out how to do things. It can be a short version of the answers to questions that your customers ask or links to a blog that deal with an issue.

Social media can be used to build a buzz when you're launching new products or services or to promote special offers.

It can also be used to get feedback and opinion on specific issues or products.

Who are you really?

Jokey names are not appropriate for business use and, if employees already have personal accounts using unprofessional names, you may need to ask them to create a new account that they can use in connection with the business.

People buy people so hiding behind a pseudonym isn't recommended. If your staff are representing your organisation, then you are being reasonable when you ask them to be up front, real and professional.

This might include specifying that people must complete their profiles properly – if there is no content, no photo and no information – people won't take your staff seriously. Including things like – how to optimise your Linked In profile in your social media training will make a big difference.

Review before you hit *Send*

There are two sides to this – the professional and the personal. It's obvious that when someone is representing their organisation they should be expected to be careful of what they post on social media. However, some people forget that, even on their personal accounts on Facebook, Linked In and other platforms, they have their employer listed. Everything they post can be connected to their current employer.

Nobody wants to have an employee who has been branded a loose cannon or hothead – and, if their posts refer to their work at all, this can reflect on the organisation.

Individuals do have the freedom to express themselves online – but they must also be conscious that, whether they intend it or not, everything that they say can be linked back to the organisation they represent professionally.

There is actually a word that means 'to lose your job because of what you have posted online'; it's *dooced*[21]. Nobody wants your staff to be on the firing line, so ensuring that there is some guidance on what the organisation considers acceptable – and not acceptable – is essential.

Who is listening?

With the theory of six degrees of separation in mind any person in your organisation could reach anyone in just a few tweets or Facebook posts. Whereas at one time it would have taken some time to reach someone who was in the fifth or sixth 'circle'; today millions of people can see a tweet within a matter of minutes.

What you say in the pub no longer stays within those four walls. In seconds your comment can be broadcast to millions of people worldwide by smartphone, sometimes with deadly effect.

This means that there is a high likelihood that former, current and future clients, employees and suppliers will see any posts that are made. We're not advocating monitoring every post, but we do believe that educating your staff about how to present their thoughts is a positive way to deal with the issue of upsetting people unnecessarily.

Walking the legal tightrope

With the wealth of information published on the web it can be easy to overlook the need to acknowledge when other people's work is quoted.

If your employees are referring to a blog, article or website ensure that they always check for copyright and attribute appropriately. It will save you embarrassment and the receipt of nasty legal letters!

---

[21] This is an American word, but we thought it was interesting that someone has actually coined a word to describe this.

Some people have been asked for their Facebook log in information at interviews in order to allow employers to see what kind of posts and activity they have on social media.

Some employers do actually require new employees to sign a 'non-disparagement agreement'. We're not promoting this – however, it does need to be clear what is and is not acceptable.

Transparency v confidentiality

Nobody wants to hide the organisation behind a lot of smoke and mirrors – transparency is important to enhance your reputation as an organisation that does what it promises in a straightforward, honest and visible way.

However, every organisation has information that needs to remain confidential. Whether that's processes, ingredients, components, manufacturing secrets or other information that would be considered to be confidential.

It's important to ensure that over-enthusiastic members of staff don't post confidential information at any time, even if it's unintentional. Without proper guidance it can be all too easy for individuals to give away trade secrets

Linking to your overall policies of what constitutes gross misconduct may be necessary to emphasise the seriousness of this. Employees who share confidential or proprietary information do so at the risk of losing their job and possibly even ending up as a defendant in a civil lawsuit.

When work and social interaction collide

In any large organisation you will almost certainly have a couple of social media junkies; they're the ones that can't move without their smartphones and tweet and post whilst they're talking to you. Some employers are dubious about the wisdom of giving these people free rein to use social media at work – there's a danger that they won't actually do any work!

If you educate people about how social media should be handled for work purposes and what is acceptable in social usage, then it can actually be beneficial to the organisation.

It's important that there are guidelines and it may be that some roles lend themselves to a higher social media usage than others. For instance:

- **Customer service** – should monitor social media for mentions of the organisation so they can respond quickly.
- **Purchasing** – may find it useful for resourcing good deals and hard-to-find products or components.
- **Marketing** – will find it really useful for staying in touch with a huge base of potential clients and referrers.
- **Accounts** – probably won't want to share confidential information online so careful guidelines are needed.[22]
- **Stores** – may find it useful to contact suppliers who use social media, but need to be careful of what is said in the public domain.
- **Production** – might use it in conjunction with marketing to promote products, but would need to be careful about what information is published.[23]
- **IT** – could find it useful for researching new systems or products, but again, will need to be careful what is published; i.e. not the number of complaints resolved – you don't want people to get the idea your IT systems are subject to problems!

You get the idea!

The other side of this is that there must be some restraint about how much time is dedicated to online activity. If your organisation has role profiles based on deliverables it should be easy to tell whether people are meeting their work responsibilities or not.

If you operate with job descriptions that are task focused or a set of competencies it can be more difficult to assess, but each manager

---

[22] There have been instances where disgruntled suppliers have posted about slow paying organisations so remember that reputation can be negative as well as positive.
[23] This is a good example of knowledge information education where helpful practices are shared openly.

should keep an eye on social media usage and remind their team of the main responsibilities of their role.

What else should your online policy cover?

Your employees should understand that you can and will monitor employee use of social media and social networking websites, even if they are engaging in social networking or social media use away from the office.

Educate them properly – this means having social media training or regular social media review bulletins. You could always post a series of how-to-get-it-right videos on YouTube for your own employees – but share them with others to enhance your community citizenship!

Typically, getting people involved will help them to take ownership of their social media activity. If the management set the direction and educate people wisely, they'll become self-policing.

Here are some statements that have been included in existing social media policies:

- Sign up for any and every social media service to reserve our name
- Use company standard e-mail address and add as much of our company information (address, toll-free, fax, etc.) as possible.
- Set privacy settings to be as open as possible and still within the social rules of the community.
- Sometimes friends or connections don't want their stuff out there, so respect that.
- Sign up for e-mail notifications and RSS feeds and put them into the corporate RSS reader account.
- Never post anything you would be afraid for your Mom to see.
- Respond to all communication within 24 hours in this order: employees, old/repeat customers, vendors, affiliates, new customers, potential customers.[24]

---

[24] We don't agree with this order – this was just something that has appeared on a social media policy – we'd advise that customers should come FIRST!

- Give the customer not just information, but the power to choose how they want their problem fixed. YOU have the power to:
  - Fix any problem, in any way, immediately that costs less than $50. More than$50 and it may come out of your pocket. Reviews are every week.
  - Engage customers in conversations where they are happening. You're representing us and we trust you: act accordingly.
  - Word of mouth is extremely important to us. If you can make the experience better than expected, do it.

Social media induction

When you launch your social media policy and, thereafter, when new people join your organisation, it's essential to have an induction that demonstrates what is encouraged and how they can help the organisation.

Part of that induction will also flag up what is not encouraged and what will end up with the individual undergoing disciplinary processes – or worse still – ending up in court! However, the emphasis should be on the positive side of social media and could include:

- Examples of posts that are helpful.
- How to generate value based posts.
- How to interact online with customers.
- How to respond to enquiries
- Examples of personal posts that impact on the organisation (positively and negatively).
- Platforms that the organisation wants to be active on; platforms where the organisation doesn't want to be involved.
- How to get video posts approved for loading on the company channel.

Every organisation is different and the induction process will need to be developed to meet specific requirements.

Multi-site/multi-national management

The first issue to resolve is that when you're dealing with several different places, there are more opportunities for misunderstanding, so it's important that everything is crystal clear. Where multi-national organisations are involved social media policies must take into account different cultures and not ask people to behave in a way that is contrary to their beliefs.

The challenge of developing a social media policy for a multi-site organisation is that it can end up with several parts of the organisation contributing to the requirements. This can end up with complex result that nobody understands.

Ideally, one person will be given responsibility for developing the policy with input from departments – marketing, HR, sales, operations, etc. – and also from country managers to ensure that it doesn't cut across cultures.

PETER'S STORY

Inchcape Fleet Solutions Portsmouth is a Positive Ground client and found that the company intranet provided information, but not communication. They realised that they needed something that fulfilled that need and we created a closed Facebook user group for 180 people for internal use only.

This created a social community which people used to exchange views, information and was much more informal than dedicated e-mail. Their group used the skills of 25-35-year-olds who were already good at social media and helped to develop some of the older team members who had only dabbled in social media.

There were a few older people who got involved – notably the Board – and a few younger members of staff who were technophobes and didn't want to participate.

Our take was that it was likely to be an 80:20 split and, currently, it's close to that.

Because it was for internal use only it created a chatty, informal arena for the whole internal community. People chose whether to be involved or not, however, as it has become established more people have dipped their toes into the water. It has improved relationships as well as the community as a whole.

The ability to apply Facebook security settings has protected each individual's privacy by allowing people in the group to see only the part of the profile that the user wants to be visible.

Posts are not confined to business, which has been a contributory factor in people getting to know their colleagues better. However, because it's a company forum, people tend to post appropriate content even when it's social.

Communicating with clients and gaining new customers

We've already mentioned that many large organisations use social media to monitor customer issues so they can respond quickly, but many large organisations send customers to their Facebook page instead of to their official website, simply because it allows them to communicate.

Social media can reduce stressful phone calls and allow organisations to be much more proactive in solving problems. It enhances their profile, saves money, is more efficient, much more friendly and allows them to interact with customers in their preferred media.

If someone mentions your organisation on Twitter or Facebook, responding to it promptly makes a big difference.

This quote from a Carphone Warehouse customer demonstrates what is possible:

'...in desperation, I turned to Twitter to try to penetrate what felt like the huge, uncaring behemoth of Carphone Warehouse. And I found Guy Stephens, the company's knowledge and online help manager, who appeared to be tackling customer rage in a passionate, empathetic manner on Twitter.

I tweeted him at 8pm. By 8:07pm he replied. I was unconditionally blown away. Three months of torturous phone calls with the contact center had gotten me nowhere. But via social media, I felt listened to within minutes and my problem was solved within a few days.'

Facebook, Twitter and even the more formal Linked In are all more accessible than hanging on the phone for hours waiting for customer service to kick in.

Monitoring social media allows you to search for specific key words and phrases and this means that, when someone is searching for what your organisation provides, it's easy to connect with them and start a conversation. This can reap rewards as this shows your organisation to be proactive and helpful, winning lots of brownie points when that person makes the decision about which organisation they want to deal with.

THE POINT OF THIS CHAPTER
Managing your reputation online

As a large organisation it's essential you put a social media policy in place so that everyone knows what is expected and acceptable. This will stand you in good stead as your staff learn to use social media to promote the organisation and provide information that builds a great reputation.

To do this it's important to educate staff properly so that they are competent in social media as they are at the other skills associated with their role in the organisation. They need to be competent at not just one social network, but all the ones where the organisation is active and wants to develop a profile. This might include Twitter, Facebook and Linked In, and also the newer sites like Google+ and Pinterest.

If your organisation is on several sites and/or across more than one country then it's essential to take into account the cultures and ethnicities of the staff in all locations when developing your social media policy.

If you get all of this right you can find you have a powerful tool to build internal relationships, world-class customer service and generate potential business from other social media users.

A single lie destroys a whole
reputation of integrity.

BALTASAR GRACIAN

CASE STUDY – INCHCAPE FLEET SOLUTIONS

Inchcape are a worldwide organisation with many divisions. The activities of any part of the organisation that bears the 'Inchcape' name will, inevitably, impact on all the other divisions by association. This means that the whole organisation has to be conscious of the responsibility they have towards their sister divisions.

Inchcape PLC has a social media policy that applies to all divisions and Inchcape Fleet Solutions has developed their own social media strategy in context with the group policy. Currently this is being used internally, aligning their activities using the group policy as guidance.

Within confines of policy, colleague guidelines have been constructed to provide advice to employees on appropriate representation, both of themselves and of the organisation. This includes reference to personal usage to avoid personal and company embarrassment. Although social media is currently only being used internally, the social media policy embodies the required and desired behaviours that reflect the organisation's culture, ethos and beliefs.

"Inchcape are exploring social media carefully to ensure that corporate social media usage is planned and done well. The intention is to use it to engage with customers and as part of the organisation's marketing, but with so many divisions it will have to be managed and the necessary resources developed," says Paul Serrell-Cooke, Programme Change Manager.

Across the UK individual centres have Facebook Pages where they interact with customers and in varying degrees they may use it as a subtle marketing tool.

Overall the organisation is cautious about social media and well aware of the pitfalls that it can create, which is why they are taking it slowly.

Paul observes "Although there isn't a policy on using search engines and social media to check people out who are coming to meetings or interviews, many of the managers do this informally and find it a really useful tool. In fact, in a recent meeting one of the people attending informed me that he had looked me up on LinkedIn. I was pleased that he had made the effort to get an idea of who I was and learn a bit about me."

Inchcape PLC are conscious of the impact of all their activities and do have a clear policy on who talks to the media and represents the organisation in public as well as what should be said. The policy has clearly laid down procedures as to how to direct enquiries from the media to ensure a consistent message.

This is delivered through an education process that ensures that everyone is delivering a consistent image both internally and externally.

More about Inchcape can be found on their website: http://www.ifs.Inchcape.co.uk.

CHAPTER 11

Reputation management for social enterprises

When you're running a social enterprise there are many more elements to take into account when you're developing your reputation.

You're going to have lots of competition as there are dozens of charities all needing to raise money and keen to get people's attention. Unlike profit-based models the majority of funding for social enterprises comes from donations of some kind or government or other funding, adding another dimension to how the business runs. Charities are always looking for innovative ways to source the funding they need and now have to compete not just locally, but nationally and internationally.

Even if your social enterprise has a sales model included where goods or services are sold in return for money, there is still a need to get the goodwill of people willing to donate, get involved with fundraising or include legacies in their wills.

Social enterprises need to be run more like a business as government and corporate funding has been slashed as the economic situation globally has bitten hard. The credit crunch also means that people have less cash available to donate and they are more careful about handing out the odd fiver here and there.

This means that your reputation needs to be very high profile and also to present your image in a way that is clear and compelling.

It's also essential that your reputation is protected and maintained. This can be harder to do when you are dependent not only on your staff to promote your interests, but also a diverse band of volunteers and supporters. The phrase 'herding cats' comes to mind!

Induction for all

As a social enterprise you will have several different groups of people to take into account.

- Your **staff**, who form the backbone of your organisation – and may be in one or more locations.
- Your **volunteers**, who you rely on for support in a wide range of activities, from envelope stuffing to speech making.
- Your **trustees**, who are often a diverse group of people who come together to set the direction the organisation takes, but may be from many different backgrounds.
- The general **public** who support you by attending events, donating money or getting involved in fund raising events.

Unlike a corporate organisation, you will need to have induction processes for staff, trustees and volunteers. It's easier to develop an induction for people who are on your payroll, but a tough tightrope to walk for people who are giving you their time. Whilst they have the best interests of your organisation in mind when they sign up, it only takes one disaffected individual to chatter indiscriminately about an office conflict, internal issue or challenge facing the organisation to create a very visible problem.

This means that a policy will need to be developed to protect your reputation in the local community, at events, with the press and, in today's world, on social media.

The induction process will need to include education on:

- The image that you want to project and the pitfalls that staff, volunteers and trustees need to be conscious of.
- Internet usage and how social media is used
- Out of office behaviour, not only when representing the organisation, but to create awareness that what you say and do, even privately, can impact on the organisation.
- Individuals will be affected by the politics in the social enterprise and, where this reaches the public arena, they can be affected by their association as volunteers. They need to know how to deal with this, should this arise.

You are likely to have a high percentage of your volunteer team in the older age group, as retired people have more time to give. Some of these people will be less computer literate than younger volunteers, but many 60+ people have had to use computers in business and many have Facebook accounts to communicate with children and grandchildren.

Social enterprises tend to have a more emotional base and it's important that all the individuals who are involved understand how they can affect their chosen charity by association. It may seem obvious, but sometimes people just don't think about it and making them conscious of the issues helps them to be careful of what they do and don't say.

Educating everyone on what is and is not acceptable online is an essential part of induction and you will benefit from a clear, straightforward social media policy.

Developing a social media policy

Because of the nature of social enterprises you are dealing with a very wide audience so you really need to get the message right. Like a corporate enterprise[25] your staff need to have a clear vision of 'how we behave and interact online'.

Whilst you will find the previous chapter useful to create the basis of your social media policy there are other issues that you will need to cover.

Reporting skills for volunteers!

Local newspapers tend to be benevolent towards the charities and not-for-profit organisations in their area, but online there are no restraints, everyone can post whatever they like. Your social media policy will need to lay out exactly what you'd like people to post – and what they should guard against saying.

---

[25] You will find it really helpful to read the corporate section as a larger organisation there are plenty of useful bits of advice that you can apply.

You may have a designated PR department who do all the communication with the local and (where appropriate) national press, TV and radio – and if a volunteer is representing you at an event the reporter that attends will talk to them and publish their quotes. However, even if no reporter is there, there is nothing to stop your volunteer posting on Facebook or Twitter when they return home.

Most social enterprises will be delighted to have posts like:

Just got back from the Mytown Rotary Dinner, great that they've voted Mytown Air Ambulance their charity this year.

Or

What a buzz at Mytown Corporation! Great charity dinner and a big donation to Mytown Hospice – thanks to everyone who donated!

Or

I love being a volunteer for Mytown Children's Charity, especially when I get to collect generous donations – thanks to Mytown Lions Club.

But would be less excited to read:

Got a cheque from Mytown Rotary for Mytown Air Ambulance, but they weren't really listening to my presentation, some were asleep!

Or

Latest donation for Mytown Hospice from Mytown Corporation, a small cheque for £150.

Or

Just got back from presentation at Mytown Lion's Club; grumpy chairman didn't seem to want to part with the cheque for Mytown Children's Charity!

Your volunteers and trustees may be independent from the social enterprise, but they will be associated with it and they all need to understand the dangers of posting what may appear to be a bit of fun. Not everyone sees the funny side and comments can be taken out of context and come back to haunt the enterprise later.

Most people are aware of the danger of gossip – and online gossip can be lethal, so you need to ensure your social media policy deals with this issue.

LESLEY'S STORY

Several years ago a local charity had an incident where one of their trustees resigned. Everyone had their own idea of what happened and rumours were rife. The charity tried to keep control of the wilder speculations.

The volunteers heard about it, but although a 'don't worry, everything is under control' message was received the nuts and bolts of the situation were not clear (mainly, I believe, because the charity had some constraints from their legal department). As you can imagine this 'vague' message just cranked the gossip up a few notches.

As this was some years ago, very, very few of the volunteers even knew social media existed so the 'gossip' was confined to friends and family, I dread to think what would have happened in that situation today. Twitter and Facebook would have been buzzing with it! The world has changed and it's essential that organisations are aware of the power that everyone has at their fingertips.

Dealing with other people's comments

With any organisation that interacts directly with the local community, there will be people with opinions – who aren't afraid to air them! For example, at one time if people didn't like the latest projects that the Parish Council proposed, they would put up flyers in the local area and a few local people see them. Today's objectors post on Twitter and the whole world sees it.

It's almost impossible to prevent individuals posting what they think, but it's essential to have a monitoring system in place that allows you to know quickly when comments are posted and go to work to respond and support or explain when needed.

Part of your social media policy may need to specify whether or not you want individuals to add their comments to support the organisation or whether they should leave it to your PR department to deal with.

You may not want inexperienced people to 'muddy the waters', no matter how indignant or passionate about your cause they are.

The danger of addressing all these issues is a social media policy that becomes very complex and detailed. However, the simpler and more straightforward you can make it, the easier it will be to get the message across to everyone it affects.

Leveraging social media

Whilst you may need a social media policy that is even more nailed down, social media opens the doors to a wealth of opportunity too.

It's easy to dwell on how easy it is to get it wrong and put a completely negative spin on protecting your image, so it's just as important to highlight how people can use social media individually to help the social enterprise they support.

Social enterprises need to talk to many different groups:

- **The general public** who may donate money, carry out a fundraising activity or organise a fundraising event.
- **Local associations and clubs** that donate funds regularly to charity.
- **Local businesses** who may be willing to advertise or sponsor fundraising activities.
- **Large organisations** whose local branch may be able to provide sponsorship or support.

These means that your cause needs to be strong enough to rally people and also to reach all these different groups. Social media offers a great way to present your cause providing you manage it well.

- *Twitter* can provide short and snappy messages to engage people with low attention spans.
- *Twitter* also offers the opportunity to provide a tempting headline and link to your blog where you can layout the whole story.
- A *Facebook* Page provides a place for volunteers, staff and supporters to engage with the social enterprise.
- *Linked In* can be a valuable platform for reaching the business

community and encouraging them to get involved as part of their corporate social responsibility activities.

- *Google+* can allow you to communicate with specific circles of people – like volunteers, trustees, clubs and associations – to keep them up to date with information that directly affects them.
- *Pinterest* gives you a platform to publish your pictures of events, beneficiaries and human interest to a wide audience and visual images are very powerful.

Whatever platform you use social enterprises have an advantage over corporate in that they usually have a wealth of heart-warming stories, which are ideal for engaging people. For example:

- *Our new equipment allows therapists to help five more kids every month to live a better life. Thanks for all the donations and support.*
- *The Air Ambulance rescued a man bitten by an adder – who was allergic to the venom and would have died if they hadn't flown in.*
- *Charity Fun Run raised £23,000! Thank you everyone who took part or sponsored a runner.*

Social media gives you the platform for making your own news and reaching people who might otherwise never hear of you.

It's a great way to get people behind a specific project – more people signing up to do a sponsored walk, run, abseil, parachute jump, slim, cycle ride or dragon boat race.

Social media has the ability to reach much further than your local press and you don't have to hit a slow news day to get published. You can present yourself in the way you want to and as often as you wish.

Good use of social media can really level the playing field for smaller charities. If you want to get your social enterprise a higher profile, clever use of social media can make a significant difference to your reputation and profile.

Many social enterprises don't use social media as well as they could so if you embrace it you are likely to be ahead of your competition. However, it does have to be planned and have a strong strategy underpinning it.

Your reputation and the money issue

One of the biggest challenges that social enterprises have – and more so since the advent of the credit crunch – is that they have to talk about money a lot. Big charities can get celebrities on board and get donations from people who don't have a regular giving habit.

Children in Need and Sport/Comic Relief get high profile time on radio and TV every year with a host of big name supporters asking everyone to give. The sums raised are astronomical by most people's standards and run into millions. However, whilst it sounds like a lot, many people don't realise how much even their local charities need to stay afloat.

Social media is an excellent platform to educate people about the costs of running your charity. This might be done as a series of posts on 'Did you know ...' lines. For example:

- *Did you know that XYZ charity gets NO funding from the government?*
- *Did you know that it costs £250K every month to keep our Air Ambulance flying?*
- *Did you know that a donation of £10 a month will pay for an hour of hospice care for a sick child?*[26]
- It can be used to get people involved in fundraising. For example:
- *Who do you know who wants to lose weight? Get them motivated with a sponsored slim*
  http://www.linktopageonourwebsite.com
- *Great day out on Sunday15th at Grantley River Park – come and cheer the Dragon boats on and support XYZ charity too.*
  http://www.linktopageonourwebsite.com
- *If your club is looking for a charity to support – find out about how we support you in return.*
  http://www.linktopageonourwebsite.com

---

[26] These are not actual figures, just examples.

As long as you don't overdo it, people pass on this kind of thing if they think they are helping a good cause. It often triggers ideas and people get involved where they might not have thought of it otherwise.

THE POINT OF THIS CHAPTER
Managing your reputation checklist

Think about the challenges that all the different groups of people involved with your social enterprise are likely to pose.

Ensure you've got a sound induction process that addresses issues that may seem obvious, but are often overlooked – until they become a problem.

Develop a sound social media policy – and educate your staff, volunteers and trustees in applying it.

Encourage the use of social media to promote your activities – teach your team to be reporters with a positive spin.

Remember that social media is a great way to educate and also to fundraise.

For the first time in my life, I put my body and reputation on the line to stand up for my beliefs and do the right thing. I hope I've encouraged other people to do the same.

LUCY LAWLESS

CASE STUDY – ESSEX AND HERTS AIR AMBULANCE TRUST

The Essex Air Ambulance Charity was created in 1997 to raise the funds for an Air Ambulance for Essex. In 2007 they took on the fund raising for a helicopter for Hertfordshire and raised the funds to launch the Herts Air Ambulance in 2008.

Whilst the charity is inspiring, Chief Executive Officer Jane Gurney, is very aware that their reputation is very precious.

'The more I've seen, the more I've learned. I've noticed other people get into situations that have affected their reputation, without even realising it's happening to them. It makes me reflect on how we're seen and to have things in place to ensure we can deal with any issues well.'

Jane's strategies include ongoing dialogue with the senior management team and the Board of Trustees about what is going on and how the Trust deals with issues that arise. The culture is transparent and, when challenges arise, action is taken quickly.

A recent PR landing of the helicopter caused an issue with someone locally, who complained about the disruption. The Trust reacted instantly by contacting the person (by a member of the management team) and apologised, inviting them to come and meet the crew, and find out more about the charity.

'I've learned you can't leave things or have a long process for dealing with people. It just makes the problem worse. We need to react honestly, decently and quickly. We don't get it right all of the time, we're human, but, when we are wrong, we apologise and try to set things right – and learn from it. If we don't learn from it, we've failed.'

The Trust has recently developed a social media policy. They are aware of the many challenges they face in managing this. Jane herself has educated her friends not to post photos and comments on Facebook that may have an impact on the Trust's reputation.

'Now they send me the photo by e-mail,' she says.

Some of the people who work with the Trust are volunteers, which makes managing their activities harder than for most organisations. However, their enthusiasm for the charity combined with a continuous process of education about how the charity wishes to be presented to the public, ensures that they don't post inappropriate comments online.

The communications team have a plan, they tweet and post on social media to keep people informed about events and engaged with the charity. Some of it is information; some is fun – like the caption competition, the latest batch of doughnuts that have arrived at the office and other fun stuff. These posts get a massive response from people, but are still controlled and monitored.

Jane admits that she uses social media for business purposes.

'If I'm meeting someone I will look them up on Google and check their social media profiles out. We do it for new staff and volunteers too.'

Even though the volunteer base tends to be older people who have retired and have more time to give to the charity, it's no longer an assumption that they are unlikely to be computer literate. Many of them are retired business people who have used computers every day of their working lives.

The Trust's Communications Team is responsible for handling all the media contacts – both online and with the press. Every member of the Trust's team has been trained to respond to requests from the press with 'That's fantastic, we'd love to chat to you, here's the contact details for the Comms Team ...' Even Jane herself consults with them before she makes any presentation to ensure that she covers the right issues and then she puts her personal spin on the presentation.

The same applies to the Trustees – communications are routed through the Chairman, but their individual expertise is shared when needed, just not without consultation first.

'We have policies and procedures. Even if the worst should happen and we have an incident, there is a plan that includes who speaks to the media, what the key messages are and how it's dealt with. It's not random or luck, it's planned and everyone has been trained,' explains Jane.

The volunteers and staff all receive a handbook and training. This explains what is acceptable and why it's important. The emphasis is on the fact that everyone is working with the charity for the right reasons and nobody wants it to suffer.

The Trust has a fund raising department and it's part of their brief to network with business people and other organisations locally to raise awareness. They are refining their networking plan so that they have a consistent image across both counties and reach as many people as possible.

Jane has had a business mentor for several years and has recently started working with a new one. She is very aware of the challenges she faces – especially as she has recently taken on the lead communications role in the Association of Air Ambulances to pull the group together.

'Everyone is at a different stage of the air ambulance journey, so it's challenging to create a common perception,' she comments.

However, she is aware of her responsibilities, having joined the charity nearly 10 years ago and having held various positions before being appointed Chief Executive Officer.

'It's really important not to believe your own hype; many high profile figures have lost sight of their impact on the world and ended up in the danger zone. You need to remember you're only as good as your last gig.'

Jane sees herself as part of a dedicated team of staff, trustees, contractors, volunteers and supporters. Her role is to coordinate it all.

'It's been both brilliant and challenging and I never forget it's a real privilege to look after our helicopters and clinical service that helps keep it flying and saving lives. To do that we have to keep our positive image – and whilst it's inspiring to save lives, it's also easy to fall from grace.'

Find out more about the Essex and Herts Air Ambulance Trust at http://www.ehaat.uk.com/

Section 3

HOW TO CREATE A GREAT REPUTATION

CHAPTER 12

Opportunities to enhance your reputation

Throughout this book we've talked about how you represent yourself and your business, with the focus firmly on networking, both offline and online. These methods offer you an active way to develop your reputation and build your authority in your niche.

This chapter will take a look at some of the other – sometimes less obvious ways to enhance your reputation.

Everything you do to market your business, your services and your products has an impact on your reputation. Choosing your marketing tools and the arenas in which you're active can make a big impact on how you're perceived.

Advertising

This isn't for everyone – some businesses don't find advertising is the right medium for their business – but if you go down the advertising route, you do need to choose your media carefully.

Consider who is reading or viewing your chosen channel – is this group likely to have a high incidence of your target market?

Many people decide that, because they are a locally-based business, they should advertise in their local newspaper. However, they don't consider whether their potential customers read that paper or not.

I was working with a newspaper in the Middle East and the Production Manager was complaining that he wasn't getting the response he'd hoped for from an ad he had placed in The Times (the UK newspaper) for a Deputy Production Manager.

I asked him why he had chosen The Times to advertise and he said 'Because they've got a really good recruitment section.'

'But are the readers of The Times all qualified to be the Deputy Production Manager of a daily newspaper?' I asked.

'No, but a lot of people read it so some of them must be qualified,' was his response.

I asked if there was a professional publication that covered the industry that people who would be appropriately qualified read. He received one of these himself – but they didn't have a recruitment section. I suggested that they might take his money if he asked if he could place a quarter page ad – and that might cost less than a much smaller ad in The Times!

His argument was that the readership of The Times ran into hundreds of thousands and the professional journal's readership was only a few thousand. However, when he realised that a very high percentage of these readers would be suitable applicants, he rethought his strategy!

What is the moral of this tale? It's better to be highly visible in a small pond made of up your target audience, than almost invisible in a huge lake populated by lots of people who are mostly not interested.

Choose your advertising media carefully and you may very well discover that not only are you reaching the right people, but advertising may also cost you less when your message is going to fewer people.

Your website

In today's world most businesses have a website – this is somewhere that people go to check them out. Whether you've got great search engine optimisation so that you appear high on the rankings or just have an active social media profile and network well offline, your website is likely to be the point at which people decide 'Yes, this seems like a good outfit' or 'No idea what this is all about, not worth dealing with'.

Your website needs to:

- Look professional – first impressions count.
- Have a strong message that's easy to understand – people are lazy and can't be bothered working hard to find out what's on offer.
- Be easy to get around and find stuff – most web surfers are impatient, if they can't get what they want quickly they just go somewhere else.

The right website can be as good as a professionally-produced brochure.

Marketing material

Everything that you hand out or send out to people that represents you and your business has an impact on your reputation. This includes your business card, flyers, brochures and leaflets.

We've already covered business cards at length and mentioned marketing material in the sole consultant, small business sections, but we make no apology for repeating some of this advice – even larger organisations have been known to get it wrong.

Brochures should be professionally produced. This means that they need to be professionally:

- Designed
- Written
- Printed on decent quality paper that reflects your image.

Far too many small businesses create DIY brochures on their inkjet printers on 80gsm paper that look cheap, lightweight and amateur. None of these words are words anyone wants associated with their business!

It's worth the investment – or maybe, if your budget doesn't stretch to this, delaying production until you can afford it or finding another way to present your business.

Do you really need a brochure? Would a business card followed up by a friendly e-mail and a professionally-constructed proposal do the same job?

If your website presents you professionally, you could direct people there instead.

The same applies to your flyers and leaflets. It's tempting to just run a few off for a networking group meeting – but, if your networking group operates properly, those flyers may end up in the hands of some very high profile clients. What might they think about the quality of your service or products based on what they have in their hands?

Even larger organisations are occasionally guilty of doing a rush job on last minute flyers for an event or offer. It's not that they don't have the budget, more that they don't have the time and a garish flyer stuffed with information doesn't hit the target – and is often inconsistent with their image.

Market carefully and think before printing.

The other give-away items are promotional gifts. We all have coasters on our desks branded with someone's marketing; or notepads, mugs, paperweights, pens and other items that someone has given us at an event or as a *Thank you for being a client* gift.

These are great ideas, but must match your company's brand and quality standards.

─────── LESLEY'S NOTES ───────

I have two coasters on my desk right now – they both have messages:

Coaster 1: Our service is what sets us apart from the rest. With phone, e-mail, website and logo.

Coaster 2: We make signs... accompanied by logo, telephone and website.

It's interesting that both messages are about them – and not about what I get as a customer – they both make me want to say 'so what?'

They're both good quality – the first a wipeable, hard plastic and the other a cork-backed, leather effect (better than one I was given recently that appeared to be cardboard and, when damp, the printing rapidly came off!)

Whatever your chosen promotional gift it must be good quality and must deliver a strong message for the recipient.

Networking

There is a host of face-to-face networking opportunities[27]. It's easy to get drawn into membership of a local group only to find that they don't reach your market effectively.

Do your homework[28] and find out not just who the members are, but how successful the members are at reaching your target market. You can ask the group leader or chapter director or organiser – and, if they don't know, ask them to refer you to someone who does. A good networking group should have either statistics or anecdotal evidence based on actual events.

Try a few groups as a guest and pick the ones that seem most connected to *your* audience.

Become a presenter

We're not suggesting you become a professional speaker, but that you learn to do short presentations to small groups to help people to understand what you do. It's not everyone's cup of tea, but if you can do a 10-15 minute presentation around your expertise, you'll have a powerful means of enhancing your reputation.

Your local networking groups are good places to start as most of them have short speaking opportunities – you just need to know their criteria.

Once you've gained confidence then there's nothing to stop you offering to present at other groups. People always want a good speaker and if you can offer interesting subject matter many institutes and associates will be eager to have you come and present to their group. It's a great way to talk to group of people who either are your target audience or are a direct route to your target audience.

---

[27] You'll find lots of networking information in *...And Death Came Third*
[28] Another good read if you want to really get your networking activities working is Recommended by Andy Lopata.

Support a charity

There are all kinds of benefit to supporting a charity. However, if you choose to do this, you need to do it because you believe in the charity, not just because it's good press.

There are advantages – but they all have a cost.

- If you actively support a charity, you'll share their press coverage (and local press tend to have a benevolent approach to charities so they generally get good coverage). However, you will have to invest time and effort in providing the support they need.
- Your chosen charity can be a great way to give the staff a common focus; however, if they're involved in fund raising events, most of it is likely to be on company time.
- Whilst you can share the charity's limelight – they'll expect to share yours too! So expect to add their name and logo to your corporate stationery, website and press releases.
- You can't pick up and drop your charity support when it suits you. If you make the commitment when your business is in a quiet period, you'll still have to make the time to meet your commitments when it's a busy time.
- Choose a charity that you believe in and also one that fits with your business. You wouldn't support an animal rights charity if your business sells leather products, for instance. The message must be consistent.

Sponsor an event

Event sponsorship can be expensive – big organisations have their name attached to huge international events and pay millions for the privilege – unless you choose carefully.

Sponsoring the County Cricket Ground so it becomes the Ford County Cricket Ground is not within most people's budgets, but sponsoring a roundabout might be more affordable.

Local Councils are always looking for ways to keep their costs down with everyone complaining about hikes in Council Tax so they often have schemes to involve local businesses. These often involve things like flowerbeds, park benches, roundabouts, hanging baskets in the shopping centres – all the things that cost the Council money.

Having your name on something highly visible locally – and being attached to an environmentally friendly activity is usually good for business.

You can sponsor or co-sponsor a local event – or create one of your own. We've seen

- Sponsored quizzes in the local shopping centre
- Sponsored walks or runs
- Sponsored shows
- Sponsored high street events (like the Christmas lights or Summer Fayre)
- Sponsorship for a local sports person or for items of their kit

These all offer opportunities to be seen as a supportive member of the local community and raise your profile. However, you do need to think about these things before choosing – if your business promotes eco-friendly products, sponsoring the local GoKart Champion may not enhance your reputation!

On the other hand if you are clever your sponsorship can make a huge impact and get you additional press coverage. For instance, the lighting company that sponsors environmentally friendly Christmas lights!

When you sponsor something be sure to remember to promote it in all your networking activities online and offline too.

THE POINT OF THIS CHAPTER
Putting it all together

Be creative about how you develop your reputation.

Be willing to share your knowledge and network discerningly.

Choose activities that you can maintain and will genuinely add to your reputation (and help you and your staff to be proud to support them).

The next – and final chapter – will help you to pull all these issues together to create something that works for you. Nobody expects you to do everything, but you do need to think about whether all the things you do are enhancing your reputation.

The danger is always in those activities that you do without thinking – that, in hindsight, haven't done you any favours. We hope that this book has, at the very least, made you think about all aspects of your activities, personal and business. The saying goes 'You don't know what you don't know'; the aim of this book is to ensure that you *do* know and can make informed choices as a result.

Get your pen out – you'll need to make notes as you read the final chapter!

Entrepreneurs are risk takers, willing to roll the dice with their money or reputation on the line in support of an idea or enterprise. They willingly assume responsibility for the success or failure of a venture and are answerable for all its facets.

VICTOR KIAM

CHAPTER 13

Your reputation action plan

So how do you practically implement a system to measure and develop **your** reputation?

Positive Ground uses a checklist to work through their clients' current activities and to create a plan of action to improve and manage their reputation. These are the main areas that you'll need to address.

How serious are you?

The title of this book may be *The Reputation Game*, but, in business, creating, maintaining and protecting your reputation is far from a game.

Your reputation has a direct impact on the success of your business; if your reputation is damaged, your bottom line will take a hit. Customers are fickle and it doesn't take much for people to lose faith in their current supplier and 'defect' to a competitor.

In order to ensure your reputation remains unsullied you need to have your wits about you and to take positive action. Whilst a reputation can be developed over a period of time, it can be lost in a heartbeat. If you've read Section 1 of this book you should be only too well aware of the fragility of any individual's or organisation's reputation.

If you really understand the risks of losing your good reputation, you'll be ready to do whatever it takes to safeguard it and put in the effort to make your reputation strong. This will ensure that people talk about you and your organisation with respect and confidence.

Have a strategic Reputation Day

This is a self-examination process to establish where you and your organisation are currently.

Start with the business:
- How do you perceive its reputation?
- What indicators are you using to make you come to that conclusion?
- What activities will support a positive reputation?
- What activities might put your good reputation in jeopardy?

Ask other people how they perceive your organisation:

- What do your employees think – and what makes them feel that way?
- How do your suppliers see you? Are you a 'good' customer? Why do they think that?
  - Do you order well ahead of time or are you a last minute-in-a-panic company?
  - Do you pay on time?
  - What kind of relationship do you have? Can you discuss problems with your suppliers and be confident that they will support you when necessary?
- What do your clients see?
- What kind of words and phrases do they – or would they – use to describe your organisation?
  - Successful
  - Easy-to-deal with
  - Helpful
  - Innovative
  - Take time to understand – and solve – their issues
  - Highly competitive
  - Low cost
  - Cheap and cheerful
  - Premium offering
  - Worth every penny
  - Feel like you're part of their team
  - OK – but would move for a better deal.

- How do your prospects respond to your organisation's name and what is their perception of your reputation?
  - Well-known in your area
  - Well respected
  - Think you're expensive
  - Keen to work with you
  - Known for going the extra mile
  - Great reputation for delivering every time
  - Liked by existing clients
  - Heard nothing but good about you
  - Have heard one or two mildly disturbing stories, but nothing to substantiate them
  - Know lots of people who rave about how good you are
  - Have seen enough material to be confident that you know your stuff.

Don't forget to include what your industry thinks.

Competitors talk and, whilst there are a few who will bad-mouth you, the ideal situation is to have competitors who respect you and who would be willing to refer clients on to you, if they can't do the work themselves. Are you at the top of their list?

When you've done this exercise for your organisation, repeat it for yourself. Whether you're:

- An independent consultant, speaker or trainer.
- The owner of a small business.
- An MD, CEO or Board member of a larger organisation.
- The manager of a department.
- A COO or Trustee of a social enterprise.

Your personal reputation will have an impact on your business, associates, clients, customers, staff and investors.

If you're serious about your business, you had better be serious about your personal reputation. As many high profile people have discovered, there is no such thing as a 'secret'. Sooner or later, there will be a leak and information you had hoped would never see the light of day will suddenly be in the spotlight.

It's better to be aware of your reputation and nurture it to avoid the discomfort of any shortcomings being revealed in all their grubby glory!

What methods of communication do you use?

Communication is an essential tool. Despite people talking a great deal about intuition, you cannot rely on the people around you practising telepathy and clairvoyance!

The way in which you communicate with your team, your clients, the people you hope will become clients, your suppliers and the rest of your industry says a great deal about you and your organisation.

There are plenty of 'corporate' jokes and cartoons about poor communication – and it's just as important with a handful of staff as with a large corporation.

Just for starters consider how you communicate:

- Your business objectives to your staff, associates and contractors, so that they understand not only your aspirations, but also their own role in achieving these. Understanding and involvement creates commitment.
- The value of your clients or customers to your organisation so that they are treated well by your staff and each client feels important as a result.
- Your ethos, values and beliefs to prospective clients to give them confidence that they will receive a first class service, plus honest and prompt information if problems arise.
- Quality and integrity to the others in your industry so that you develop a well-deserved reputation for being reliable, honest and trustworthy as well as for delivering a first-class service or product.

Don't forget that – as a leader – your personal approach to communication will filter down through your organisation. It's not something that you can 'stick on' later – you need to start as you mean to go on. This means that, even if you haven't got any staff right now, you should establish a means of communicating with clients, suppliers, prospects and your industry that can be passed on to employees in the future, or to associates and contractors, if you outsource work of any kind.

LESLEY'S STORY

I was discussing communications and development with a client some years ago. They were a small insolvency practice with 14 staff. The owner was raving about how great his staff were and how hard they worked.

I asked him what the company objectives were and he talked about aiming to turn companies around first if at all possible; treating his clients to an occasional 'jolly' and, eventually, promoting his great team as the company grew.

I asked if he had these objectives written down.

'I don't need to,' he said, 'it's all in here.' He tapped his temple knowingly.

I asked him how his team helped him with achieving these objectives. He looked at me in astonishment. 'They don't need to know,' he said, clearly surprised that I should think that they would be involved.

'How can they help you to achieve them, if they don't know what they are?' I asked.

'They just do their jobs,' was his response.

Frankly, I was astonished that they were all performing as well as he said, as they must have had little idea of the impact of their activities on the success of the organisation.

Do you cover all the bases?

The success of this exercise depends on you considering your reputation from every angle – and all the activities, attitudes and approaches that contribute to it.

Look at every aspect of your organisation:

- Management at every level
- Marketing
- Sales

- Finance
- Purchasing
- Customer service
- Production
- Maintenance
- Human resource management.

If possible get your team involved – in fact, if you're brave enough, get some of your valued customers and suppliers involved too. Most of us are too close to our own business to see it objectively. A fresh pair of eyes is invaluable.

Develop a programme that will enhance and grow your reputation

There are a number of stages to this programme. They need to be considered, planned and established as part of your organisational culture i.e. how we do things around here.

1. What activities are already in place that you want to maintain or increase?
   a. What do you want the results of these to be?
   b. How will you test and measure the results?
2. What activities are already in place that you want to change or stop (and why)?
   a. What will have to happen to get these to change or stop?
   b. What are the danger signs of them reappearing?
   c. What can be done to encourage people (including yourself) to change the existing habit(s) for new ones?
   d. What monitoring system will need to be in place to support people through the change process?
3. What new activities need to be developed?
   a. Who is responsible for strategic development of the programme
   b. What needs to be invested – time, money, people, skills, resources – to set these up?
   c. Who is responsible for the day to day operation and achievement of objectives?

d. Who will be responsible for carrying them out?

e. How frequently will each activity take place?

f. What are the measurable elements that will indicate success?

g. How frequently will they be tested and measured?

Ensuring the message is received and understood

Whilst you may imagine that, because people have the power of speech and can hear, they also understand and can translate your objectives and plans to the team they manage. This is usually not the case at all!

When you're a larger organisation two problems can occur:

1. The senior management team presents the corporate objectives to their team – in their original form. The challenge is that, what makes sense at board level is often perceived by more junior staff as 'nothing to do with me'.
2. The Chinese Whispers effect may come into play, where the message changes on the journey through various levels of management.

Consequently, it is essential that every manager and supervisor knows how to 'translate' the message into 'what that means to me' for each member of their team. This will impact on skills required, prioritising activities, understanding the outcomes needed, level of commitment – and the customer experience.

When you're a sole trader, independent consultant or SME there's less chance of the message getting mangled. However, even small businesses have been known to fail to communicate their core message accurately to associates, suppliers and those people in their network – so don't skip this activity.

This all impacts on your reputation, so it is essential that you find a way to articulate your expectations and objectives in simple language and in bite-size chunks. We find that the Reputation Matrix we outlined in Chapter 6 is a brilliant way to communicate these messages.

Education for the future

How will you ensure that you and your employees continue to see this as essential to success?

If you are changing existing habits and putting new activities into place it's easy to slip. Once this starts to happen there's a danger that someone will write off all these uncomfortably different ways of doing things as 'not working' and they will get abandoned.

To protect you and your organisation, it's really important that you establish a system and process that enables you to get right back on track, even if things get in the way here and there.

The other part of this is to educate your people thoroughly as to how they each affect your organisation's reputation and what they can do to ensure that they work for, or with, an organisation that is highly respected, a good employer, and is profitable and growing.

As we've already said – if people understand what you're trying to achieve and feel a part of the process, the commitment levels soar.

You might encourage your team to think about their own personal reputations and what they can do to ensure that they get good press. In fact, you could even give them a copy of this book to read!

THE POINT OF THIS CHAPTER – AND THIS BOOK

How serious are you really?

If you've got to here then you're in a hurry to get started or you've diligently ploughed through the whole thing! However, reading a book is not enough. The fact that you know a lot about developing, maintaining and protecting your reputation won't help you unless you take action.

What are you going to do now? It doesn't matter what, it just matters that you do something positive that will:

- Enhance your reputation.
- Help you to become more respected.
- Give you the status of being the first person people suggest when anyone asks 'Who do you know does (whatever you do)?'

If you just think 'that was interesting' and put this book on your bookshelf, we've failed!

Like most people, we want to succeed – and for us to succeed, you need to succeed too – in building a brilliant reputation and making sure you keep it that way.

So – how serious are you about managing YOUR reputation?

At ev'ry word a reputation dies.

ALEXANDER POPE

The Authors

Lesley Morrissey

Lesley is director of Inside News Limited and has worked with companies who have a high regard for their reputation for nearly three decades. Nine years with Dubai Duty Free were an education in reputation marketing and this has been equally important in her roles with smaller enterprises like Attitudes in both Dubai and the UK.

As a Reputation Marketing specialist Lesley works with driven entrepreneurs with a vision, helping them to be visible, to look good and build a first class reputation as a leader in their field.

Her commercial writing skills and marketing knowledge, particularly online, provide the support and advice businesses need to position and present their organisations on websites, brochures, newsletters and marketing material.

Lesley also runs a membership website: www.stepbystep-onlinemarketing.com providing support for business people who are just getting to grips with marketing online.

More information can be found at:
www.insidenews.co.uk
www.lesleywriter.com
www.3andahalfsteps.com
www.twitter.com/lesleywriter
uk.linkedin.com/in/lesleymorrissey/

Peter Roper

Peter provides Business Development resources through high value products, keynote speaking and consultancy. "I don't do glib theories, just practical tried, tested and proven practises that I have, in the main, learned the hard way!"

Peter had a very successful corporate career with organisations such as Lombard North Central and Arval PHH. After being awarded Sales Executive of the year for a consecutive six years, he went on to become the youngest ever Divisional Director of PHH. Peter created a strategic Division with a turnover in excess of £38m, employing over 200 people and winning numerous national awards.

From 1996 Peter became a serial entrepreneur and has had six family businesses, three huge successes that are still flourishing and three fantastic failures – all of which helped his learning curve to rise rapidly. Peter together with his co-author Andy Lopata became Amazon #no 1 bestselling authors in 2006 with *And Death Came Third!* the definitive guide to networking and speaking in public. Peter is known as The Natural Speaker and during his career has spoken to over 500,000 people and in several countries.

In 2010 he launched his personal story in the acclaimed book *Running On Empty* – thirty seven mistakes **not** to make in business!

In 2012 he was voted Motivational speaker of the year by the PSA. Peter has been a board member of the PSA since 2009, National President 2010 and made a trustee of the PSA Foundation in 2013.

In 2013 Peter became become the chief editor for the FAMILY Business Owner Magazine, a publication dedicated to helping family owned and operated businesses.

Peter's vision: *Family Businesses Matter!*:

"My goal is to help as many family businesses to be successful, not just financially, but as families. After all isn't that why the business exists – to help the family?"

For more information go to:
www.familybusinessman.com
www.facebook.com/peterroper1
www.twitter.com/fambusinessman
uk.linkedin.com/in/peteraroper/